Fifty Shades of
Grammar

Arlene Miller

The grammar DIVA

Other books by Arlene Miller:

The Best Little Grammar Book Ever: 101 Ways to Impress with Your Writing and Speaking

Correct Me If I'm Wrong: Getting Your Grammar, Punctuation, and Word Usage Right

Beyond Worksheets: Creative Lessons for Teaching Grammar in Middle School and High School (e-book, with homeschool adaptations)

The Great Grammar Cheat Sheet: 50 Grammar, Punctuation, Writing, and Word Usage Tips You Can Use Now (e-book)

The Best Grammar Workbook Ever: Grammar, Punctuation, and Word Usage for Ages 10 Through 110

Fifty Shades of Grammar

Scintillating and Saucy Sentences, Syntax, and Semantics from
The Grammar Diva

Arlene Miller

THE GRAMMAR DIVA

bigwords101
Petaluma, California

Fifty Shades of Grammar: Scintillating and Saucy Sentences, Syntax, and Semantics from The Grammar Diva

Copyright © 2016 by Arlene Miller

Cover concept by Arlene Miller and Matt Hinrichs
Cover design by Matt Hinrichs
Interior formatting by Marny K. Parkin

Publisher's Cataloging-in-Publication Data

Miller, Arlene.

Fifty Shades of Grammar: Scintillating and Saucy Sentences, Syntax, and Semantics from The Grammar Diva, First Edition, 2016

ISBN 978-0-9911674-2-5

1. English language—Grammar. 2. English language—Usage. 3. English language—Grammar—Self-instruction

Library of Congress: PE 1106.M550

Dewey: 428.2

Published by bigwords101, P.O. Box 4483, Petaluma, CA 94955 USA
Website and blog: www.bigwords101.com

Contact Ingram or the publisher for quantity discounts for your company, organization, or educational institution.

THE GRAMMAR DIVA

As always,
To Jake and Shelley
my two greatest loves

Contents

My Gratitude

Thank you to everyone who has been on this amazing journey with me. For as long as I can remember, I have wanted to write a book. About eight or nine years ago, shortly after I became a teacher, I decided to write a grammar book that compiled all the most common errors people make. At that time I outlined a book, which I finally wrote and published about five and a half years ago.

Two years later I wrote another grammar book. Then, I gathered together some of the grammar lessons I came up with for my own classes and put them together in an e-book. A couple of years ago I wrote an even smaller grammar e-book. Recently I wrote and published the grammar workbook I had wanted to write for a long time.

My latest offering to you is a compilation of blog posts from *The Grammar Diva* blog, which I have been writing since the beginning of 2013. I couldn't possibly list all the people who have been on this journey with me, but here are some to whom I give my gratitude.

This book wouldn't exist without these three people: Gil Namur, the keeper of my website, who taught me how to write the posts on my site and how to send them out and share them with everyone; Marny Parkin, who designed the interior of my first book as well as the workbook and this book; and Matt Hinrichs, who has designed most of my book covers.

And thank you . . . Bobbi and Dave Noderer (old friends), Edie and Jim Partridge (old friends), Frances Caballo (new friend), Jeannie Thomas (new friend), Norma Sadow (old friend), John DeGaetano (biz manager), Maureen Richardson (who looked at my finances and told me "failure is not an option").

Elaine Smith, Marie Millard, John Lehmann (retired principal), Robin Kneeland (teacher), Jon Day (teacher), Michael Powell (librarian), Pete Masterson (print maven extraordinaire), Joel Friedlander (mentor), Linda Jay (colleague), Judy Baker (who helped with the subtitle of this book), Linda Reid (friend and mentor extraordinaire), Sue Behrens (linguist and colleague), Jeff Deck (typo hunter), Benjamin Herson (typo hunter), Jeane Slone (book distributor extraordinaire).

Sheri Graves (writer), Robin Moore (writer), Susan Littlefield (writer), Kay Miller (writer), Marilyn Campbell (writer), Waights Taylor (writer), Gordon Burgett (niche writer extraordinaire), Amber Starfire (writer), Lee Foster (travel writer), Mark Coker (mentor, Smashwords owner), Ransom Stephens (writer), Ronn Owens (KGO radio host), Ray Lawrason (Copperfields Books), Grace Bogart (Copperfields Books), Dr. John Walker (principal), Dr. Tim Nonn (former reporter), Susan Bono (writer/publisher), John Crowley, Yovanno Bieberich (reporter), Frances Rivetti (writer), Nancy Cordova (colleague), Michael Marcus (colleague), Mignon Fogarty (The Grammar Girl), the seventh grade students I taught for eleven years . . . and so many more.

Thank you.

Introduction

Around the time I was finishing my first book—that would be early 2010—I started thinking about beginning a blog. I don't know if it was my own idea or if someone told me that authors should have a blog. As usual, the technical aspect of it stopped me for a few years.

Finally, I found a real web designer and got a Word Press website on which I made a blog page with complete instructions from my web guy on how to write a post and send it out. Thank you, Gil Namur.

I started my blog at the beginning of 2013 and have faithfully posted every weekend since. My blog has become *The Grammar Diva Blog*. Although I do blog about grammar, I also blog about the language, punctuation, words, social media, technology, education, and other related topics. I hope my posts are interesting, informational, inspirational, and instructive—although maybe not all at once!

Thank you to all of you who may have subscribed to, read, and commented on my posts. I have selected fifty of my favorites for this book and have divided them by topic. I have grammar posts, punctuation posts, my collection of holiday posts, posts about words and the language, a few quizzes, some posts I couldn't fit into a category, and finally the Fifty Shades of Grammar series, which began when I asked my readers for their grammar-related pet peeves.

Please relax with a cup of coffee, tea, or whatever, and enjoy . . .

Part One

Grammar Posts

1. *Who* and *Whom* Made Easy

(3-2-13)

I recently read that people have finally just given up on learning the difference between *who* and *whom*. Lazy, lazy, lazy! What is this language coming to, asks this grammar hawk! It appears that it is now "semi-OK" to just use *who* and not worry about it anymore. For example: *Who are you going with?*

It isn't hard at all to figure out which to use: *who* or *whom*.

Here it is, easy as pie!

Substitute *he* and *him*. If *he* works, use *who*. If *him* works, use *whom*. It's easy to remember because both *him* and *whom* end with *m*. If it is a question, you will have to turn it into a statement or answer the question.

Examples:

- ***Who/whom*** are you going with? I am going with ***him.*** So, use ***whom!***

- Do you know ***who/whom*** is standing there? ***He*** is standing there. Use ***who.***

- I know ***who/whom*** you are talking about. You are talking about ***him.*** Use ***whom.***

You will never have to wonder whether to use *who* or *whom* again. I think they all gave up much too soon! ✎

2. *Me, Myself,* or *I?*

(4-17-13)

My newest pet peeve is the incorrect use of the pronoun *myself*. I have been hearing it more and more often—or perhaps I have just noticed it more often. I hear it on the news, in conversation, on television—everywhere. I imagine that people use *myself* when they can't figure out if the correct word is *I* or *me. Myself* also sounds more erudite, so perhaps that is why people tend to use it.

Myself (along with *yourself, himself, herself, itself, ourselves,* and *themselves)* is called a **reflexive** or **intensive** pronoun. The other such pronouns don't seem to cause trouble—just *myself.*

Here is an example of *myself* used correctly as a **reflexive** pronoun:

- I wrote that proposal *myself.*

Here is an example of *myself* used correctly as an *intensive* (showing emphasis) pronoun:

- I *myself* wrote that proposal.

Here are some examples of *myself* used incorrectly:

- He gave my friend and *myself* some new books.

- My neighbors and *myself* are having a party next weekend.

- Joe read the letter to my sister and *myself.*

Okay. So when is it correct to use *myself?*

Fortunately, this is an easy rule to remember. In the first **correct** example, *myself* bounces back (as in *reflexive*) to the *I* at the beginning of the sentence (which is the subject).

In the second **correct** example, the *myself* emphasizes (as in *intensive*) the *I* at the beginning of the sentence (which is the subject).

In the incorrect examples, the subjects of the sentences are *he, my neighbors,* and *Joe,* respectively.

You got it! You CANNOT correctly use *myself* in a sentence unless *I* is the subject! ✎

3. *Which. That. Who.* Help!

(5-25-13)

I have been asked to write a blog post about *which* and *that*. Frankly, I would prefer to avoid that issue altogether and do something more enjoyable—pulling weeds or cleaning my house, for example. But here goes . . .

Which, who, and *that* introduce adjective clauses, which describe some noun in the sentence, usually the once preceding the clause. Here are some examples:

- My uncle, ***who works in Hollywood***, is coming to visit. (describes *uncle*)

- The kids ***who are standing on the corner*** go to my school. (describes *kids*)

- The dress ***that is in the window*** is beautiful and very expensive. (describes *dress*)

- My car, ***which is in the garage***, needs new brakes. (describes *car*)

- The tribes ***that live in Connecticut*** are listed in Chapter 7. (describes *tribes*)

But now . . . when do you use *which*? *that? who?*

And when do you use a comma around the clause and when don't you?

Allow me to explain:

- *Which* is generally used for things and animals, not for people.

- *Who* is always used for people.

- *That* can be used for people or things, but is generally used for things. *That* can be used for species or types of people.

Examples:

- The **car, *which*** is in the garage, needs new brakes. (thing)

- My **uncle, *who*** is an actor, is visiting next month. (person)

- The **book *that*** is on the table is a bestseller. (thing)

- The **tribes *that*** live in Connecticut are described in Chapter 7. (type of people)

OK. Now, why are there sometimes commas around the clause and sometimes not?

Commas are used around **nonessential** clauses. These are clauses that could be left out without affecting the meaning of the sentence. The words in the clause are added information.

There are no commas around **essential** clauses. These clauses cannot be left out because they limit the noun they are modifying. For example

- The kids ***who are on the street corner*** go to my school. (The clause ***who are on the street corner*** tells which kids. You need that clause in the sentence, so you do not use commas around it.)

- The kids on the street corner, ***who go to my school,*** are drawing on the sidewalk. (The clause ***who go to my school*** is added information. We already know which kids you are talking about. The clause can be thought of as "by the way, they go to my school.")

Notice that for essential clauses (where there are no commas), *that* is generally used for things. However, for nonessential clauses (where the commas are used), *which* is generally used for things. For example

- The book ***that is on the table*** is due at the library.

- That book, ***which I really enjoyed,*** is due at the library.

Who can be used with both essential and nonessential clauses. For example

- My brother, ***who goes to college in Georgia,*** is coming home for the summer.

- The boy ***who is making the speech*** is the valedictorian. (We need the clause to identify which boy.)

Exceptions? Of course! You can sometimes use *which* without the commas (nonessential clauses). Examples:

- She is taking the clothes ***which fit her the best*** and ***which don't wrinkle.*** (If there are two nonessential clauses in the sentence, ***which*** is often used to introduce them.)

- That is a book **which everyone should read.** (If **that** is already used at the beginning of the sentence, **which** can be used.)

Note that is it **not** wrong to use *that* in the above two examples.

So . . . to sum up:

1. *Who* is used for people.

2. *Which* is used for things.

3. *That* is usually used for things, but can be used for people, especially for types or groups of people.

4. *Who* is used both with and without commas (that is, for both essential and nonessential clauses).

5. *Which* is usually used with commas (added information).

6. *That* is usually used without commas (limits what is being talked about and usually is necessary for the meaning of the sentence). ✎

4. If I Were in a Subjunctive Mood

(7-20-13)

Verbs are active little things. If you have been hiding under a rock and don't know what a verb is, it is an action word like *jump, think, write, read, eat, hide* . . . or a state of being like the verb *to be* (and its forms: *are, am, is,* etc.).

Verbs, of course, have **tense,** which tells you when something happened. *I am running* (present tense) indicates a different time than *I was running* (past tense).

Verbs also have **voice: active** or **passive.** When a verb is used in the active voice, the subject is performing the action of the verb. When a verb is used in the passive voice, the subject is not doing anything. Here are examples:

- **Active Voice:** I am driving to the mall.

- **Passive Voice:** I am being driven to the mall.

Verbs also have **mood.** There are three moods:

- **Indicative** is the usual mood. (Don't worry about this one.)

- **Imperative** is the command mood. (Don't worry about this one either.)

- **Subjunctive** is the other mood, You might have to worry about this one.

Subjunctive mood is used for sentences that express *demand, request, necessity, urging, resolution, wishful thinking, and improbability.* Generally, we use the subjunctive without even thinking about it. It is only the last two (wishful thinking and improbability) that trip us up—that is, if we are native English speakers. I can see where the other uses would be problematic for those whose native language isn't English (although other languages have subjunctive mood as well).

All right, already! Can we have some examples here? Of course.

- Demand: **I insist that *I be* allowed to go!** (not that *I am* allowed to go)

- Request: **The parents have asked that they *be notified* if Johnny fails a test.** (not that *they are* notified)

- Necessity: **It is necessary that *I be* given enough money to cover expenses.** (not that *I am* given)

- Urging: **We strongly suggest that Johnny *be given* an A on his report card.** (not *is* given)

- Resolution: **It was decided that *I be* the chair of the decorations committee.** (not that *I am*)

The above examples are all in subjunctive mood.

Okay. Those were pretty easy, and I am sure you use them without even thinking about it. Of course, you can use the other verb (in parentheses), but it has a different meaning, and will not imply demand, request, necessity, urging, or resolution. For example

- I told you that *I am allowed* to go out on Friday nights. (no demand here)

- The parents *are notified* every time Johnny fails a test. (no request here)

- I hope that *I am given* enough money to cover expenses. (no necessity here)

- Johnny *is being given* an A on his report card. (no urging here)

- *I am* the chair of the decorations committee. (no resolution here)

The verbs in the above sentences are **indicative mood.**

Wishful Thinking: This is one of the subjunctive uses that confuses us. Whenever you use *wish,* you need to use the subjunctive mood.

Examples:

- I wish *I were going* to Paris with you. **Not** I wish I *was going* to Paris with you.

- He wishes *he were* taller. **Not** He wishes he *was* taller.

Improbability: This is the other subjunctive use that can be confusing. When you use an *if* or *as if* clause, use the subjunctive if the sentence implies improbability.

Examples:

- If *I were* you, I wouldn't go to Paris in the winter. **Not** If *I was* you, I wouldn't go to Paris in the winter.

- She acted as if *she were* the boss. **Not** She acted as if *she was* the boss.

Many people do not use the subjunctive mood with *wish* and *if* these days, but it **is** still correct. Other tenses and verbs, of course, also take the subjunctive, but it is the examples above that are the most tricky.

*If I **were** a rich man, da-da-da-da-da-da-da-da-da-da-da-da-da . . .* ✎

5. How to Write Possessives

(8-16-13)

Possessives are one of the three **cases** in the English language (the other two are **nominative** and **objective**, but let's not worry about those!). Latin has five cases, and some languages have seven or eight, so we are doing well here. In any *case* (pardon the pun), possessives imply ownership.

We all learned in grade school that to make a noun possessive, we add an apostrophe and an *s*. Not wrong, but not the whole story.

The only words that can be made possessive are **nouns** and **pronouns**. People have difficulty with both. Just remember that **no** possessive pronouns have an apostrophe! Here are the possessive pronouns:

- First person singular: *my, mine*
- Second person singular and plural: *your, yours*
- Third person singular: *his, her, hers, its* (without the apostrophe)
- First person plural: *our, ours*
- Third person plural: *their, theirs*

Okay. Now on to the nouns.

Generally, for singular nouns you add an apostrophe and an *s* to make them possessive:

- *This is Mary's book.*

- *My dog's bowl is empty.*

- *Your essay's introduction is very good.* (Doesn't need to be a person to be a possessive.)

Plural nouns that don't end in an *s* are also made possessive by adding an apostrophe and an *s*.

- *The children's playground is across the street.*

- *The mice's home is in that hole in the wall.*

Plural nouns that end in *s* (which is most of them) are made possessive with the addition of only an apostrophe.

- *Her two sisters' bikes are in the driveway.* (One sister's bike; two sisters' bikes)

- *The parties' themes were both tropical.* (One party's theme; two parties' themes)

Most singular nouns that end in *s* or *ss* are made possessive by adding an apostrophe and an *s* (yes, really!)

- The *bus's* tire is flat. (Think of how you would pronounce it. It is spelled exactly as you would say it.)

- My *boss's* desk is really messy. (Once again, that is how you would say it.)

- *Thomas's* new car is over there. (You wouldn't pronounce it *Thomas new car,* would you??)

- I had to memorize Frederick ***Douglass's*** speech. (Yup!)

- The ***princess's*** slipper fit perfectly.

Now, lets talk about a few of those words made plural.

What if you had two bosses, and they both had messy desks? My ***bosses'*** desks are really messy. (You have used the plural of *boss,* which is *bosses,* and you have added just an apostrophe, like in other plurals that end in *s.* Once again, that is how you pronounce it. You don't add another syllable. You don't say *bosses's,* so you don't spell it that way either. My *boss's desk* and my *bosses' desks* are pronounced exactly the same way, even though they are spelled differently—because one is singular and one is plural.)

What if there were three princesses whose slippers all fit perfectly? Same as bosses. The three *princesses'* slippers all fit perfectly. (You make princess plural by adding *es,* and you add an apostrophe like in plurals that end in *s.* Once again, *princess's* and *princesses'* are pronounced the same way, although they are spelled differently because one is a singular possessive and the other is a plural possessive.)

All right. Let's do the other three examples:

- All the ***buses'*** tires are flat. (***Bus's*** is singular possessive; ***buses'*** is plural possessive)

- The two Thomases' last names both begin with ***L.*** (Correct, but you might just want to rewrite it!)

- Well, there is only one Frederick Douglass, so I guess we can't do that one!

Exceptions? Well, of course!

If a word ends in an *es* that sounds like *ez,* you just add an apostrophe to make it possessive—no *s.* For example:

- Socrates' (possessive), Hippocrates' (possessive)

- Also, the possessive of ***Jesus*** is ***Jesus;*** and I would suppose ***Moses*** is treated the same way. ✎

6. Don't Dangle Your Participles!
(8-22-13)

Waiting for the bus, the time went by slowly. You might read that sentence and not notice that anything is wrong with it. But read it again and you will see that it makes no sense—and is in fact ridiculous. We probably read, write, and speak such sentences frequently without even noticing what they really say! We call this particular error a *dangling participle*. They are best avoided! The way to avoid writing them is to know what they are, to be careful, and to proofread your writing.

The sentence above likely is supposed to mean that time passed slowly for the person waiting for the bus. But is that what the sentence says as it is written? No. It says that the *time is waiting for the bus*. Why does it say that? Well, in the English language, words are assumed to go with other words or phrases that are near them. Since *time* is placed right after the **participial phrase** *waiting for the bus*, it is assumed that they go together and that *waiting for the bus* describes the word *time*.

Let's start out by defining what a **participle** is. You know what a verb is. A verb is usually an action word of some kind, even if it isn't a physical action (for example, *think, wonder, assume,* and *determine* are not physical actions, but they are verbs). A participle is called a **verbal**—it used to be a verb, but it is now an **adjective.** An adjective is not an action word; an adjective describes a **noun** (person, place, thing, or idea) or a **pronoun** (*I, me, you, they, he*, etc.).

A participle comes in one of two types: **present** or **past.** So we need to take a verb and add something to it to make it an adjective. To make a **present** participle, we add *ing* to the end of the verb. To make a **past** participle, we use the past tense form of the verb (often an *ed* ending, but not always).

Here are some **present** participles in sentences:

1. The ***growling*** dog tried to bite the child. (The participle *growling* comes from the verb *to growl,* but is now an adjective describing *dog.* (Note that in the sentence **The dog is growling at the child,** *growling* is no longer a participle; *is growling* is now the verb. You can tell because there is no other verb in the sentence, and sentences all need verbs.)

2. I saw a ***dancing*** elephant at the circus. (The participle *dancing* comes from the verb *to dance,* but is now an adjective describing *elephant.*)

Here are some **past** participles in sentences:

1. Skating on a ***frozen*** lake can be dangerous. (The past participle *frozen* comes from the verb *to freeze* in its *present perfect* form—the form you would use with "has," "have," or "had." It is now an adjective describing *lake.*)

2. The ***burned*** building was unrecognizable as the school that it once was. (The past participle *burned* comes from the verb *to burn* in its *present perfect* form—the

form you would use with "has," "have," or "had." It is now an adjective describing *building*.)

When we use a participle in a *phrase* (a few related words strung together) to begin a sentence, we might run into trouble with **dangling participles.** (However, it doesn't have to be a phrase, and it doesn't have to be at the beginning of the sentence, as the examples below will show.) Since the participle or participial phrase is an adjective, it is thought to describe whatever noun or pronoun comes right after it. Therefore, **you want to make sure** that when you are writing, you place whatever that participle or participial phrase is describing, or modifying, **directly after the phrase!**

Here are some goofs!

- *Reading the newspaper by the window, my cat jumped into my lap.* (*Who* was reading?)

- *Growling, I fed my hungry dog.* (*Who* was growling?)

- *While still in diapers, my mother remarried.* (*Who* was still in diapers?)

- *I saw the beautiful red tulips running down the street.* (*What* was running down the street?)

- *Freshly painted and waxed, I picked my car up from the shop.* (*Who* was freshly painted and waxed?)

There are usually several ways to correct a sentence. Here is one way to correct each of the above examples. In these "fixes," the sentence was rewritten without participial phrases.

- While I was reading the newspaper by the window, my cat jumped into my lap.

- Because my dog was growling from hunger, I fed him.

- My mother remarried while I was still in diapers.

- I saw the beautiful red tulips as I was running down the street.

- My car was freshly painted and waxed when I picked it up from the shop.

You *could* rewrite the sentences keeping the participial phrases, but the rewrite might be awkward or change the meaning of the sentences, so it isn't necessary to keep the structure the same. Here are the "fixes" using the same participial phrases:

- **Reading the newspaper by the window, I was surprised when the cat jumped into my lap.**

- **Growling, my hungry dog was finally fed.**

- **While still in diapers, I saw my mother remarry.**

- **Running down the street, I saw the beautiful red tulips.**

- **Freshly painted and waxed, my car looked great when I picked it up from the shop.**

It is easy to correct the mistakes once you notice that your participle or participial phrase is dangling and doesn't make sense. One way to find these mistakes is to carefully proofread your writing!

There are other things in sentences that can also be misplaced, but that's another blog post!

There is actually a distinction between **dangling** and **misplaced** participles, although both are incorrect. A dangling participle doesn't actually describe anything in the sentence. A misplaced modifier describes something in the sentence, but not what it appears to be modifying.

- ***While still in diapers, my mother remarried.*** Dangling. The sentence doesn't say who was still in diapers.

- ***I saw the beautiful red tulips running down the street.*** Misplaced. *Running down the street* describes *I*, not the *tulips*. ✎

7. Do I Feel *Bad*? or Do I Feel *Badly*?

(10-11-13)

Many people are confused about *bad* versus *badly*—and for that matter, *good* versus *well*. *Bad* is an adjective; *badly* is an adverb. *Good* is an adjective; *well* is an adverb.

So . . . do you feel *bad* or *badly*? *Good* or *well*?

Let's start a few steps back. **Adjectives** (one of the parts of speech) are generally used to describe nouns. They tell what kind, which one, or how many. For example

- **pretty** dress (what kind?)

- **bad** dream (what kind?)

- **seven** books (how many?)

- **this** tree (which one?)

Adverbs (another part of speech) are generally used to describe verbs. Many times (but not always), adverbs end in *ly* and are formed by adding the *ly* to an adjective.

For example: *quick* (adjective) and *quickly* (adverb); *soft* (adjective) and *softly* (adverb); and *bad* (adjective) and *badly* (adverb). Adverbs tell when, how, and to what extent.

Here are some examples of adverbs in action:

- He dances **well** (how)

- He will go **soon** (when)

- He is **too** thin (to what extent—an adverb modifying the adjective *thin*)

Most of the time adjectives are placed before the noun they modify in a sentence. For example

- **I have three** (adjective) **wishes** (noun).

- **I bought the blue** (adjective) **dress** (noun).

However, sometimes adjectives appear away from the noun or pronoun they modify. For example

- The dress is **blue.**

- I am **quiet.**

- Joan is **intelligent.**

In the above examples, *blue* describes, or modifies, *dress*; *tired* describes *I*; and *intelligent* describes *Joan*.

Now, look at these sentences, which are structured in the same way, but use adverbs instead of adjectives:

- Joan speaks **intelligently** (adverb).

- I walk **quietly** (adverb).

- The dress fits **perfectly** (adverb).

In the above sentences, the adverbs describe the verbs (as adverbs usually do): speaks how? (intelligently); walk how? (quietly); fits how? (perfectly).

Now, look at these sentences:

- **The pizza looks good.** (*Good* is an adjective describing *pizza.*)

- **The man looks at her carefully.** (*Carefully* is an adverb describing *looks.* Looks how?)

- **The fabric feels soft.** (*Soft* is an adjective describing *fabric.*)

- **The woman feels the fabric lightly.** (*Lightly* is an adverb describing *feels.* Feels how?)

Okay. Let's explain all this. If you look at the first pair of sentences, with *look* as the verb, you will discover that there are two kinds of *look.* In the first sentence, no one is looking at anything. Pizzas don't have eyes. The *looks* verb here is not an action verb.

Now look at the second pair of sentences. In the first sentence, there is also no action. The fabric has no fingers, and it isn't feeling anything. However, in the second sentence, the woman is feeling using her fingers.

Some verbs (most verbs) are action words even if they represent mental action (*think, consider, wish*) rather than physical action. However, some verbs do not represent action at all. They represent a state of being, an emotion, or a sense. These verbs are often called **linking** verbs. However, some verbs can be both action and state of being, depending on how they are used in the sentence (*feel, taste, sound,* and *grow,* for example).

Linking verbs include the following (not a complete list):

- to be (is, am, are, was, were, will be, has been, have been, etc.)

- look

- sound

- taste

- feel

- seem

- become

- grow (The tomatoes are growing quickly—action; I am growing tired—linking)

If this were a math lesson, the linking verb would be an equal sign:

- I am tired. I = tired.

- Sue is tall. Sue = tall.

- The pizza looks good. Pizza = good.

If you try this with an action verb, it doesn't work:

- I play chess. I = chess? No.

- She walks the dog. She = dog. No.

Now, what does this all have to do with *bad* and *badly*, you ask? After a linking verb, you use an adjective, not an adverb. (The grammatical term for this adjective is **predicate adjective**). *I feel bad* is correct because feel is a linking verb here. To say *I feel badly* would imply that *feel* is being used as an action verb. In other words your fingertips are not working, so you *feel badly*!

What about *I feel good*? Or is it *I feel well*? Grammatically, it should be *I feel good*, since *good* is an adjective and *well* is an adverb. However, in this case (yes, there is always an exception), you can correctly use *well*, because *well* has been accepted to mean a state of good health. So, either way, you are correct.

Now, **I feel bad** if I have confused you, but **I feel good** if I have helped to "unconfuse" you! ✎

8. "A" Historic Blog Post

(11-1-13)

I have been asked several times recently (mostly by writers) about using *a* versus *an*. The questions were primarily about which of these **articles** to use in front of the word *historic*. Is it *a historic* or *an historic*? They both sound all right, but are they?

Well, the old rule still applies: Words that begin with a vowel sound (not necessarily a vowel, just a vowel **sound**) use *an*. Words that begin with a consonant sound (not necessarily a consonant, just a consonant **sound**) use *a*. Some words that begin with *h*, like *historic,* have a definite consonant sound at the beginning; others, such as *honor*, begin with a vowel sound.

For some reason, both *a* and *an* sound natural with *historic* (and other similar words).

Following the rule, use **an** with *honor* (it begins with an **o** sound—the *h* is silent). However, use *a* with *historic*, since the *h,* a consonant sound, is pronounced.

These words should be prefaced with the article *a*:

- historic
- hysterical

These words should be prefaced with the article *an*:

- honor
- herb

You may notice that when you put the *a* in front of *historic,* you pronounce is as a long *a,* while in front of most words you would pronounce it "*uh.*" But pronouncing it isn't so much of a problem; that is simply the way it rolls off the tongue—which is exactly why *a* fits in front of some words, and *an* fits in front of others.

Follow the basic rule, and you won't go wrong.

What about the other article, *the*? Well, *the* goes in front of any letter. However, you will notice that there are two ways to pronounce it. One way is *thuh* (rhymes with *duh*); the other way is *thee* (rhymes with *tree*). When you put *the* before a word that begins with a vowel sound, you will automatically say *thee* because it just rolls of the tongue that way. Before a consonant sound, you will generally say *thuh.* Try saying *the* in front of *historic.* You might say it either way because, once again, they both sound okay. But you likely will pronounce it "*thee.*" Since *the* is always spelled the same, there is no problem here. ✎

9. My Three Big Grammar Peeves (This Week!)

1-22-15

As a grammar person, grammar teacher, grammar author, grammar blogger, grammar hawk, Grammar Diva, grammar prescriptivist—whatever you or I wish to call me—I obviously have a great deal of grammar pet peeves, and they change according to whatever grammar faux pas seems to be in vogue at a certain time. Right now, here are three I am grappling with!

#1 Peeve: The fact that radio personalities and their guests; respected TV news anchors; and well-regarded newspapers can't get their grammar right—and don't seem to care—is my number one pet peeve this week! The problem is rampant. Yes, of course I care because grammar is my livelihood (and without its proper use, I have no livelihood), but I also think that *these* people, above all, should be able to speak their own language correctly! Is it so difficult to say, "When I was a kid, my mom and I . . ."? So why did I hear instead on CNN, "When I was a kid, me and my mom . . ."?

I would fire them all if I could! They get paid enough to speak correctly. Aren't they getting paid to speak? Must they sound like morons? Do they think it's cool to sound stupid?

#2 Peeve. The improper use of myself. I am getting tired of hearing this one. People obviously think it is high-class to use *myself* as much as possible—or they don't know whether to use *I* or *me*, so *myself* seems like a good solution. Wrong.

1. **My colleague and *myself* are doing a presentation tomorrow.** Wrong.

2. **The important assignment was given to my colleague Bill and *myself*.** Wrong.

3. **I hope you join bestselling author Joe Schmoe and *myself* for this important interview.** Wrong.

Try taking out the other person. Does *myself* make any sense at all?

1. ***Myself* is doing a presentation tomorrow?** No.

2. **The important assignment was given to *myself*?** No.

3. I hope you join ***myself*** for this important interview? No.

The rule is simple: *Myself* is never the subject of a sentence, and it generally can't be used at all unless the subject of the sentence is *I*.

#3 Peeve. The whole pronoun situation: *I* and *me*, *him* and *her*, *he* and *she*, *they* and *them*, *we* and *us*. I would add *who* and *whom*, but let's not get carried away with our expectations!

It isn't rocket science. It isn't difficult. The same people saying, "When I was a kid *me and my mom would* . . ." would never say, "When I was a kid *me would* . . ." So, I am not quite sure why it becomes so difficult when the other person is added. That's why I think these people, who should know better, just think it is cool to sound like a 7th grader (my apologies to 7th graders). Likewise, he didn't give it to *Bob and I* because he wouldn't have given it *to I.* We all know the trick of just taking the other person out to see which pronoun fits.

Grammar-wise, here is the rule: Certain forms of pronouns are used for **subjects**. Subjects **do** the verb or action in the sentence and are generally at the beginning of the sentence—and before the verb. These pronouns are *I, we, he, she, they,* and *who.*

Other pronouns **receive** the action of the verb, either directly or indirectly, or come after prepositions. They are called **objects**. These pronouns are *me, us, him, her, them,* and *whom.* For example

- He kicked **me.** (Direct object of the verb *kicked.*)

- He gave **me** a kick. (Indirect object of the verb *gave.*)

- He gave a kick **to me.** (Object of the preposition *to.*)

Now I know you all have grammar peeves of your own, and I would love to know what they are, so I can write a blog post about them.

Maybe it is actually rocket science. . . . In that case, I am raising my prices! ✎

10. Your Top Ten Grammar Peeves

(1-31-15)

In last week's post I talked about my top three grammar peeves. This week I don't even remember what they were, but now I sure know what yours are! I asked in my post for you to let me know about your grammar peeves . . .

The floodgates opened, especially from the social media groups I share my posts with—who are particularly interested in the English language, namely, those who teach it to either native speakers or English language learners.

The part about the pet peeves was fine. But then, as would happen, the verbal weapons began to be drawn as the **descriptivists** and **prescriptivists** said their respective piece(s). I have talked about these two terms before, but let me review . . .

- **Prescriptivists** believe that there are grammar, punctuation, and usage rules that should be followed. I stand mostly with this group.

- **Descriptivists** believe that the way people really use the language helps it to evolve, and they do not like the word *rule* at all. They prefer *standard conventions*.

Honestly, I think that both beliefs must coexist, and that language really is a combination of both. There are rules, many of them from Latin . . . and someone didn't just make them up recently. No, they are not written in stone like the laws of physics or the multiplication tables, but they still exist in most of the grammar and style books that are around.

Yes, of course, there are also regional dialects, colloquial language, and spoken language that often differs from formal writing. And, yes, language does evolve. But should we get rid of the difference between *who* and *whom* because people can't figure it out? I don't think so; and many people *can* figure it out. Should we say, *"Me and him have went to the movies,"* just because many people say it that way? I don't think so.

Talk any way you want to your friends. But if you are making an important speech to the faculty at Harvard Medical School, or you are writing an essay to get into college, or a resume, or a cover letter, I think it is better to stick closely to the "rules."

That said, I have pages of your grammar peeves. Many of them were expected; however, there were many quite unusual ones, which I will get to in future blog posts (yup, you will have to keep reading . . .)

Here are the ten that seemed to be the most popular:

1. Misplaced apostrophes. This one includes *its* and *it's* and *your* and *you're*, the two most popular peeves. People mentioned seeing things like *"your cute"* on Facebook, and I must agree. I rarely see *you're* on Facebook! Is it that much trouble to put in an apostrophe?

It's and *its* are pretty easy to remember: All contractions (two words shortened into one) have apostrophes (*I'm, don't, we'll*), but possessive pronouns never do (*yours, ours, his*). One person said, "You wouldn't write hi's, so don't write it's!" Someone else remarked about a lawyer who writes a column using *its'* as a possessive. *Its'* is not a word at all, but I have seen it being used lately.

2. Well, this one isn't a surprise. The confusion between subject and object pronouns: Between *you and I*. He gave it to *him and I*. NO-NO-NO-NO-NO-NO-NO!

It is *between you and me*. He gave it to *him and me*. Just like "*he gave it to me.*"

One of the people who responded said she heard *between you and I* on a television program, spoken by lawyers who are supposed to have gone to Harvard. Another said a student of hers said that since she heard *between you and I* on television that it was right. The teacher told her that if she wrote it on her paper, she would flunk.

3. Less and fewer was a popular peeve. Use *fewer* for items you can count: *Ten items or fewer*. (But this cookie has *less sugar*.)

Someone who wrote to me said a Columbia University professor on CNN said, ". . . less arrests and less incarcerations." She added, "My husband had to pull me from the ceiling!" I got a good chuckle out of picturing that one!

4. *I could care less*. Well, if you could care less, then you do care, so why are you even saying it? It should be *I couldn't care less*.

5. Using a pronoun after a noun: *Mr. Jones* **he** *is going.* *The teachers* **they** *are talking. The authors* **they** *are writing.* You get the picture. You don't use both the noun and the pronoun.

6. Confusing *that* **and** *who.* *Who* is used for people. *That* is generally used for things.

The boy that made the basket was the MVP. It should be *who made the basket.* (By the way, animals are considered *that,* even though we all want to call them *who.*)

7. *Should of* **and** *could of* **and** *would of.* This is still a pretty common error—actually very common. It is *have,* not *of:*

- You should **have told me,** not **should of.**

8. *Where are you at?* I am told this is more of a Midwestern thing. Although it is pretty much okay to end a sentence with a preposition these days, it is not okay to end a sentence with the preposition *at. Where are you* is good enough.

9. *These ones* instead of *these.* This one sounds like something kids tend to say. And why is *this one* okay, but *these ones* not okay? Just curious!

10. This one is surprising, but more than one person mentioned it: The use of *be.*

- It *bes* really good.

- These cupcakes *be* like the bomb!

Certainly, this use of *be* is more common in those whose native language is not English and in some dialects. The odd thing is that it is actually an almost-correct use of the *subjunctive*, which hardly anyone uses correctly! The subjunctive is used for things that you wish were true but aren't, or for demands:

I wish *I were* rich—not I wish *I was* rich. That is the subjunctive.

She demanded *that I be there* for the meeting—not *that I am there*. That is also the subjunctive.

So, *I be there* is unusual, but *He asked that I be there* is correct!

So there you have it! Your top ten grammar peeves. Oh, but there are a whole lot more . . . so stay tuned. ✎

Part Two

Punctuation Posts

11. To Comma or Not to Comma: That Is the Oxford

(2-2-13)

We invited the two supermodels, George Clooney and Tom Hanks to the party.

What's that? Read that again? When you read that sentence, it might appear that George Clooney and Tom Hanks are supermodels. Well, while some may think so, probably not. Try putting a comma between Clooney and *and.* Clearer? Should be. Now, you can tell that two supermodels were invited to the party and so were George Clooney and Tom Hanks. Four people, not two.

That comma makes all the difference. That comma is called the **series comma,** or by its more lofty name, the **Oxford comma.** It is thus named because it was first used by the Oxford University Press. It is the comma before the *and* that introduces the final item in a series within a sentence. In the United States, it is common to use the Oxford comma. And although it is obviously used by Oxford University, most of the rest of England shuns its use. Most of the time, it makes no difference whether or not you use it, and it is a matter of personal choice. Here is an example:

- The bowl contained apples, oranges, grapes, and strawberries. **OR**

- The bowl contained apples, oranges, grapes and strawberries.

Most of the time, it really makes no difference whether or not you use it. Sometimes, such as in the example at the beginning of this post, the sentence is confusing and misleading unless you use the comma. Less commonly (in my opinion, since I am pro-Oxford comma), it is confusing to use it.

Look at this example:

- Attending the meeting were Mr. Jones, Mrs. Greene, Mr. Level, the mayor, and Mr. Falk.

Those who are anti-Oxford comma would say that the comma before **and** is confusing and makes it look as though there are five people attending the meeting. They say that if you remove the comma before **and,** it becomes obvious that Mr. Level **is** the mayor, and there are only four people attending the meeting:

- Attending the meeting were Mr. Jones, Mrs. Greene, Mr. Level, the mayor and Mr. Falk.

In my (not so) humble opinion, it is confusing either way. That's what semicolons are for (well, one thing they are for): to separate the main items in a series where there might already be commas:

- Attending the meeting were Mr. Jones; Mrs. Greene; Mr. Level, the mayor; and Mr. Falk.

In the above sentence we can tell for sure that Mr. Level is indeed the mayor.

- Attending the meeting were Mr. Jones, Mrs. Greene, Mr. Level, the mayor, and Mr. Falk.

And now in the above sentence, we know that he is NOT the mayor.

However, as long as you make exceptions when your meaning isn't clear, it is up to you whether or not you use the Oxford comma. Some find that it clutters writing. (Oh, really! It is so small!)

There is no right way or wrong way. The only thing is to be consistent. Once you have decided which way you will do things within a piece of writing (with the exception of clearing up fuzzy meanings by adding it or removing it), either use it or don't. ✎

12. Quotation Marks with Other Punctuation: You Can Quote Me on This!

(7-27-13)

Quotation marks are used around the exact words someone says and around certain titles (including song titles, chapter titles in books, and magazine article titles).

Single quotes ('), as opposed to double quotes ("), are used for quotes inside of quotes and nothing else. Do not use single quotes to emphasize text (do not use double quotes either); use italics or bold for emphasis.

It is often necessary to use other types of punctuation along with quotation marks: commas, periods, colons, semicolons, question marks, and exclamation points. So which comes first, the quotation marks or the other punctuation? Well, it depends.

Here are the rules:

1. Periods and commas ALWAYS go *inside* the quotation marks. ALWAYS.

Examples

- **"Make sure you pack your summer clothes," Mom said.**

- **Mom said, "Make sure you pack your summer clothes."**

- **She said, "My favorite song is 'Somewhere over the Rainbow.'"** (Yes, even when there are three quotation marks, one belonging to the song title and the other two belonging to the whole quote. The period or comma is inside all three quotation marks.)

2. Semicolons and colons ALWAYS go *outside* the quotation marks.

Example

- **She said, "I don't know what to do"; he answered, "I don't know what to do either."** (Colons and semicolons are not used too much with quotations marks, so I wouldn't worry about this one.)

3. Question marks and exclamation points . . . WELL, IT DEPENDS. These can go either way:

- If the question mark or exclamation point belongs to just what is in the quotes, it goes inside the quotes.

- If the question mark or exclamation point belongs to the entire sentence, it goes outside the quotes.

- If the question mark or exclamation point belongs to both, it goes inside the quotes. You do not use two.

Examples

- **He said, "Who are you?"** (The question mark belongs to the quote only, and it goes inside.)

- **Did he say, "I am John"?** (The whole sentence is a question, but the quote itself isn't. The quote goes outside.)

- **Did he ask, "Who are you?"** (The quote is a question, and the whole sentence is also a question. Don't use two question marks. Use only one, and place it inside the quotation marks.)

Exclamation points are treated exactly the same as question marks.

- **He screamed, "Help me!"** (Quote itself is the exclamation, so the mark goes inside the quotes.)

- **He had the nerve to say to me, "You are ugly"!** (The whole sentence is an exclamation, but the quoted part really isn't. Mark goes outside.)

- **I freaked out when he screamed, "You are on fire!"** (Both the quoted portion and the whole sentence are exclamations. Use one mark and put it inside.)

Please refrain from using question marks and exclamation points together.

- **He screamed, "Do you know the way?"** (You don't need an exclamation point after the quotes. It already says he screamed.)

By the way, in British English, the rules are exactly the opposite, so don't say I didn't warn you! ✎

13. Dots and Lines:
Hyphens- Dashes—and Ellipses . . .
(10-25-13)

Hyphens, dashes, and ellipses are less talked about punctuation than, let's say, commas and semicolons, but they are important to use correctly, nonetheless. And actually many of us use (and overuse) the dots and lines that are dashes and ellipses.

First, let's talk about hyphens and dashes—the lines. There are three sizes of lines, all different punctuation marks with different uses. Sometimes the problem is the ability to make the different lines on your computer!

- This little one is a *hyphen*.

– This medium one is an *en dash*.

— This long one is an *em dash*.

I have a Mac. The hyphen is on the number line. That one is easy. I made the **en dash** with Option+Hyphen. I made the **em dash** (the longest one) by pressing Shift+Option+ Hyphen. You can also use Insert Symbol for the long one and just choose a long line. These symbols, of course, are in the middle of the line. They are **not** underscores (_). Some people use two hyphens in a row for an **em dash.** Often (but I could never figure out when), the computer will put them together for you. It results in a short em dash, but it works. We rarely use the *en dash,* the shorter one, for anything, so generally an *en* might substitute for an *em.* However, if your writing is being edited, your editor might fix those dashes to make them proper em dashes.

Hyphen (-). The hyphen is used to separate words; that is its only function. It separates words that don't fit on a line. This use becomes more obsolete as computers can fit the type without splitting words at the end of a line. Or, the computer splits the word for you. If you are writing by hand, make sure that words split on the end of the line are split at the syllable break. One-syllable words cannot be split, and proper nouns should not be split either.

Hyphens are also used in some words that have a prefix, where running the whole thing together might be unclear. There may be two vowels in a row. For example,

co-op is different from *coop*

However, most words like this are clear and do not need the hyphen: *cooperate, reorder, reestablish*

Some words with a short prefix still usually use a hyphen:

ex-husband

In a word's evolution, the word often starts out as two separate words (*e mail*). As the word becomes more common, it is often hyphenated (*e-mail*). When the word becomes very common, it often becomes one word (*email*).

To determine whether of not to hyphenate a word, look it up in the dictionary. If the dictionary gives you a choice, or two dictionaries disagree, choose one way and stick to it. Consistency always gives you an air of expertise!

In addition to splitting words with hyphens, you use a hyphen in some compound adjectives, **but only** if the adjective comes before the noun.

Examples:

- I like well-done steak. **BUT** I like my steak well done.
- I have a three-year-old daughter. **BUT** My daughter is three years old.

Hyphens are also used in the numbers *twenty-one* to *ninety-nine*, which are often spelled out, and in fractions.

- My piggy bank is two-thirds full.

En Dash (–). The en dash is not used very often. It is used as the minus sign in math, and it is used in number ranges. So, you will see it in indexes for sure! Examples

- pages 25–30
- Jim Jones (1825–1900) was a hero to us all.

Em Dash (—). The em dash is used (and often overused) to indicate an abrupt change in thought or to emphasize something. If the section to be put within dashes is not a complete sentence, commas can sometimes be used instead (but you cannot set off a complete sentence with commas; you will have a run on). Parentheses can also be used instead of an em dash, but are far less dramatic!

- I was looking for the cat—I hadn't seen her in over a week—when I found her in the attic.

- My daughter—looking so radiant—got married yesterday.

To make sure you have your dashes in the right place, take out the portion of the sentence within the dashes. The rest of the sentence should be a complete sentence and should make sense on its own without the words that are within the dashes.

Important note: There are no spaces before or after a hyphen, an en dash, or an em dash.

Ellipsis (. . .). The ellipsis is commonly used when something is left out of a quote to make it shorter. Just be careful that you don't change the meaning of the quote by leaving out selected material. An ellipsis is also used to indicate an unfinished list or unfinished thought at the end of a sentence.

The ellipsis is made with three periods. There is a space before the first period, a space between each of the periods, and a space after the last of the three periods if the ellipsis is in the middle of a sentence or at the end of something that is not a complete sentence. If the ellipsis is used at the end of the sentence, the ending punctuation comes after the three periods. So, if the sentence would end in a period, the ellipsis has four dots instead of three. Another form of punctuation, if necessary, instead of a period, would come after the ellipsis. For example

- The mayor said, "There is no reason to increase our taxes in this city . . . would cause the taxpayers great hardship."

- The mayor said, "There is no reason to increase our taxes in this city . . . . (There is more to the speech, but the part given is a complete sentence, so there are four periods.)

- She thought to herself, *I need to get out of this place because if I don't* . . . (There is no ending period because there is no end to the speaker's sentence. She is trailing off.)

And this is the end of this blog post . . . ✎

14. A Toast to the Semicolon!

(1-3-14)

Some people never use the semicolon; others use it often. The only thing worse than never using it is using it incorrectly! Once you read this blog post, you will never do that.

You can get by in your writing without ever using a semicolon. There is always a way around it. If you write, you will eventually have to use a period. And if you know what's good for you, you will put some commas in there too. Question marks are sometimes necessary as well. And quotation marks. And colons are often called for. But semicolons? They can be totally avoided by alternatives and rewriting. But they are so nice to use sometimes for variety—and necessity (unless you want to rewrite).

The first thing to do is to disassociate the **semicolon** from the **colon.** They don't have much in common at all and are definitely NOT ever interchangeable. The semicolon has much more in common with the comma, and is kind of a "supercomma," if you will. Colons generally announce that something is coming: they introduce lists, either vertical or horizontal, or maybe a long quote. Semicolons don't do that.

So enough beating around the bush, you say. *What do I use the semicolon for?*

The semicolon really has only two uses:

1. It is used to separate two (or more) closely related sentences.

2. It is used where a comma would be used (to separate items in a series, or to connect two sentences where there is a conjunction like *and)* if there are already too many commas, and things are hard to read.

The first use is easy. You have two sentences. You can separate them with a period. Or, you can separate them with a comma **if you are using a conjunction.** Or, if they are closely related, you can use a semicolon and forget about the conjunction and the capital letter that would start the second sentence. For example

- I am taking the train to New York. My brother is flying.

- I am taking the train to New York, but my brother is flying.

- **I am taking the train to New York; my brother is flying.**

See? Easy! Just remember to use a lowercase letter to begin the sentence after the semicolon, and don't use a conjunction. If the sentences are not closely related, stick to a period and capital letter.

The second use for a semicolon can be worked around by rewriting if you want to avoid using semicolons. Here are a couple of examples of using semicolons as "supercommas." The first is in a series. Generally, you separate the items in a series with commas, but if some or all of the items already have commas, your sentence can be confusing:

- I went to New York with my brother, Jim, Alice, my cousin, Beth, my mother, and my grandmother.

Well, *that* is a little confusing. It is impossible to tell who is who and how many people are going with you. Here is the same sentence cleared up with semicolons:

- I went to New York with my brother; Jim; Alice, my cousin; Beth, my mother; and my grandmother.

Now you know there are five people going with you. Jim and your brother are not the same person. However, Alice is your cousin, and Beth is your mother. So you are separating the big items (yes, even before the last item) with semicolons because the individual items already have commas in them.

Here is an example of a complicated compound sentence that could use semicolons:

- My company's offices are in Bangor, Maine, Manchester, New Hampshire, and Queens, New York, and the other company's offices are in Hoboken, New Jersey, Boston, Massachusetts, and Baltimore, Maryland.

Understandable if you know some geography, but so many commas! Here is a better way:

- **My company's offices are in Bangor, Maine; Manchester, New Hampshire; and Queens, New York; and the other company's offices are in Hoboken, New Jersey; Boston, Massachusetts; and Baltimore, Maryland.** (In this case, the conjunction *and* after *New York is optional;* you can use it or leave it out.)

One more example to sell you on the use of semicolons:

- **I packed the following items: two pair of pants, brown and blue, three shirts, three pair of black shoes, gray, black, and brown socks, and striped pajamas.** (Forget the fact that nothing matches!)

Let's use semicolons:

- **I packed the following items: two pair of pants, brown and blue; three shirts; three pair of black shoes; gray, black, and brown socks; and striped pajamas.** ✎

15. Colon Alert:
Something's Coming . . .

(3-20-14)

If a colon (the punctuation symbol, not the internal organ) could talk, it would say, "Pay attention to what is coming." A colon is used to alert the reader that some important information follows. Here are the common uses for the colon: (And that was one of them!)

- Used in digital time after the hour to tell you about the minutes (10:45)

- Used sometimes to introduce a quote that is a sentence or longer

- Often used between the title and subtitle of a book in text (not on the actual cover)

- Used between two sentences when the second sentence expands upon or explains the first one

- Used after the greeting of a business letter (Dear Mr. James:)

- And, of course, used to introduce a list, either vertical or horizontal

This post deals with the last one, using colons to introduce a list. First of all, forget about semicolons (;) right now; the semicolon is not used in any of the same ways as the colon. Colons (or occasionally periods, but never semicolons) are used to introduce lists.

I was once taught not to use a colon (but to use a period instead) unless the words "following" or "as follows" were used in the sentence introducing the list. Not really true. You can use a colon anyway. I was also taught at this time not to use *following* as a noun, because it is an adjective. Okay, generally true, except Justin Bieber still has a *following,* as do the Beatles. But I digress. It is true that *following* should probably have a noun after it. For example

- Please make sure you have the **following:** (okay)

- Please make sure you have the **following items:** (better)

Horizontal Lists

Use a colon in a horizontal list when the information before the colon is a complete sentence. Otherwise, there is no punctuation. Look at these two examples:

- **Please bring the following items: pen, pencil, notebook, and laptop.** (Since there is no complete sentence after the colon, no capital letter is needed.)

- **Please bring: pen, pencil, notebook, and laptop.** (This sentence is not correct. There should be no colon after **bring.** There is no stop there if you are reading the sentence, so do not put any punctuation in it.)

- **Please bring a pen, a pencil, a notebook, and a laptop.** (correct)

Vertical Lists

You have a little more leeway in a vertical list. It is still best to use a complete sentence to introduce the list if you want to use a colon. If the introduction is not a complete sentence, you don't need any punctuation. However, since the list is more separate in a vertical list than in a horizontal, you can get by with a colon. See the examples here.

Please bring the following items:
- **pen**
- **pencil**
- **notebook**
- **laptop**

Or you can say

Please bring (or **Please "bring:"** if you must)
- **pen**
- **pencil**
- **notebook**
- **laptop**

You don't use any periods after the items in a vertical list unless they are complete sentences. And if one item in your list is a complete sentence, all items should be. They should also all be written with the same structure (called **parallel structure**).

Sometimes people write a vertical list as if it were a sentence. For example

Please bring
- **a pen,**
- **a pencil,**

- **a notebook, and**
- **a laptop.**

I don't personally like this method, but it is okay to use.

Here is an example of a list that isn't parallel because one item is not a complete sentence:

In this seminar you will discuss these important things:
- **Marketing is a full-time job.**
- **You need to use social media.**
- **Proofreading your writing.**
- **Blogging is very helpful.**
- **It is important to develop your brand.**

The **proofreading** item doesn't belong. It is the only item that is not a complete sentence.

Here is another list that isn't parallel because one item is structured differently.

In this seminar you will learn
- **how to market your project**
- **how to develop your brand**
- **how to create a website**
- **blogging every day** (doesn't fit here!)
- **how to best proofread your writing**

(You could have capitalized the items in the previous list if you wanted to.)

Here are a few other tips:

- No, you don't need to use bullets in your lists unless you want to. However, they are effective.

- You can use numbers if the order of your items is important, or the number of items is important or previously mentioned.

- You can capitalize items in a vertical list even if they are not complete sentences. ✎

16. Apostrophe Catastrophes

(7-10-15)

Whenever anyone writes a post or article titled, "The Five Biggest Grammar Mistakes" or "Three Grammar Mistakes That Will Make You Look Stupid," apostrophe issues are always included. What makes this little "high comma" so confusing? Let's take a look at the mighty **apostrophe.**

There are three uses for this little mark ('):

1. Apostrophes are used in contractions to replace the missing letters. (Contractions are words or word combinations in which letters have been omitted: *can't* for *cannot, we're* for *we are*, etc.)

2. Apostrophes are used to make nouns possessive: *Mary's* hat, my *brother's* car, etc.

3. Apostrophes are **occasionally** used in plurals. Let me repeat: **occasionally.**

Of course the most common apostrophe errors are the *its* versus *it's* and *your* versus *you're* versus *yours.* Number 1 above says that apostrophes are used in contractions. *It's* is a contraction meaning *it is. You're* is a contraction meaning *you are.* Easy. When *it's* and *you're* are used as contractions, use an apostrophe.

Notice that Number 2 above says possessive **nouns,** not possessive **pronouns.** Possessive pronouns do not have apostrophes! These pronouns include *ours, theirs, his, hers, yours, whose,* and *its.* So, none of the possessive pronouns includes an apostrophe including *its.*

- *It's* means *it is:* It's raining. *Its* is possessive: The cat ate its food.

- *You're* means *you are:* You're coming with us. *Your* is possessive: I made your lunch. This lunch is yours.

- *Who's* means *who is:* Who's this person? *Whose* is possessive: Whose coat is this?

Remember: Contractions always have apostrophes to stand in for the missing letter or letters. Possessive pronouns do not have apostrophes.

Other things to remember about apostrophes:

- Apostrophes are used in possessive **nouns.** Possessive implies ownership and is not the same as plural, which means more than one. To make a singular noun possessive, we usually add an *apostrophe* and an *s.* For example: the dog's food, my mom's shoes.

- For plural nouns that don't end in *s,* also use an *apostrophe* and an *s* for the possessive. For example: the children's rooms, those women's hats.

- For plural nouns that end in *s,* just put an apostrophe after the *s.* For example: the dogs' food (more than one dog), my sisters' toys (more than one sister)

- For singular nouns that end in *s,* usually use an apostrophe and an *s,* going by the way you would say the word.

For example: Thomas's room, my boss's desk, Frederick Douglass's speech. But you would probably say Miles' room, because you might not pronounce it as *Miles's*.

- Plain old plurals generally DO NOT have an apostrophe! For example: I just posted some new photos (not photo's). The oranges are on sale (nor orange's).

- Use an apostrophe for plurals of letters, numbers, and abbreviations only if the word is confusing without the apostrophe. For example *a*'s, so it isn't confused with the word *as*. Same goes for *i*'s and *u*'s. *ABC*s does not need an apostrophe, as it is not confusing as it is. Some people like to use an apostrophe with plural numbers, but it isn't necessary: Your answer contains too many 7s. (**Note:** When you use a word or number or letter as itself—too many 7s, all *A*'s, four *i*'s in this word, too many *and*s, etc.—the letter, number, or word is in italics, but the *s* is not.

- Sometimes people, especially in informal speech, will make a noun into a contraction: That **photo's** really good. It means ***photo is,*** so it is a contraction, and you do need an apostrophe; it is not a plural.

- When you say **1960s,** there is no apostrophe.

- When you say the **'60s,** there is an apostrophe because you have left out part of the year.

There are no other uses for the apostrophe that I can think of right now. Remember: contractions use apostrophes, and possessive nouns use apostrophes. Possessive pronouns do not. ✎

Part Three

Posts About Words

17. There Is Nothing to Fear

(1-11-13)

Veering just a little bit away from grammar this time to talk about words.

Phobias

Phobia means *fear.* It is both a word unto itself and a common suffix. Some of the more common phobia words are **claustrophobia** (fear of enclosed spaces), **arachnophobia** (fear of spiders), and **agoraphobia** (fear of the marketplace, or the fear of leaving home). However, the types of phobias stretch into the thousands; it seems as if there is a phobia for almost everything. Here are some of the more interesting phobias:

Allodoxaphobia—Fear of opinions

Anablephobia—Fear of looking up

Apeirophobia—Fear of infinity

Arachibutyrophobia—Fear of peanut butter sticking to the roof of the mouth

Aulophobia—Fear of flutes

Bathophobia—Fear of depth

Bogyphobia—Fear of bogeys or the bogeyman

Chorophobia—Fear of dancing

Consecotaleophobia—Fear of chopsticks

Euphobia—Fear of hearing good news

Geniophobia—Fear of chins

Kathisophobia—Fear of sitting down

Levophobia—Fear of things to the left side of the body

Nomatophobia—Fear of names

Omphalophobia—Fear of belly buttons

Scriptophobia—Fear of writing in public

Syngenesophobia—Fear of relatives

Zemmiphobia—Fear of the great mole rat

and my favorite . . .

Hippopotomonstrosesquipedaliophobia—Fear of long words ✎

18. Can You Spell These Words?

(4-27-13)

Or—perhaps a better question to ask these days is, "Will you ever *need* to spell these words?"

Spell Check won't catch you if you make a mistake with *your* and *you're* or *its* and *it's,* but it will alert you if a word is just plain spelled incorrectly—as long as it is close enough for Spell Check to recognize! And since hardly anyone is ever away from a smart device of some type—whether it be a tablet, a phone, or a laptop/desktop—is there any reason to even learn how to spell correctly anymore?

Since we spend most of our time in places other than in dark caves, on top of mountains, and under rocks, where there may be no Internet access, is learning how to spell obsolete? Is it now in the category of typewriters and cursive handwriting?

Well, I asked you the question; I don't really have the answer. However, some people think spelling is important enough to still have national spelling bees, so perhaps spelling will become a novelty talent like juggling or yodeling.

That aside, there are words that are tough to spell. I consider myself a good speller, but there are some common words that I tend to avoid because I can't spell them.

Here are ten commonly misspelled words:

1. Probably the granddaddy of them all is ***accommodate.*** I don't have any trouble with this one. It is really pretty easy. All you have to remember is that there are two ***cc*'s,** two ***mm*'s,** and two ***o*'s!**

2. Sometimes people misspell ***misspell*!** Is that one *s* or two?? Easy one. One *s* goes with the prefix ***mis,*** which means ***wrong.*** The other *s* goes with the ***spell*!**

3. I used to be embarrassed that I couldn't seem to spell ***embarrass*!** *One r or two?* I would ask myself! I have finally learned. Two *r*'s and two *s*'s.

4. Some people get the vowels mixed up in ***relevant*** and spell it ***relavent*.**

5. Both ***conscience*** and ***conscious*** are confusing! ***Conscience*** (the one that can be guilty) has ***science*** at the end. ***Conscious*** (the one for which you might need coffee)—well, I have no hints for that one (sorry).

6. ***Believe*** is probably less confusing that it used to be. First of all, it does follow the rule of *"i before e except after c."* You can also remember to never ***believe*** a ***lie,*** and you will get the *ie* correct.

7. What is with the word ***definitely***, and why can't any of my students spell it? It either comes out as ***defiantly*** or ***definately.*** It seems as though there is always an errant ***a*** in there somewhere!

8. ***Questionnaire*** is a tough one for me. I can never remember if there is one *n* or two! And while we are at it, if you ask me, I won't be able to spell ***millionaire/millionnaire***

either! So which one is it, anyway? (Oh, Spell Check tells me it has one *n*. So why does *questionnaire* have two?)

9. *Harass* is kind of like *embarrass*. Are there two *r*'s or just one? Turns out that in *harass*, there is just one. Isn't there?

10. The tenth one is tough to pick, because there are so many to choose from! I will let you choose. Which of these words do you think is toughest to spell?

discipline? cemetery? guarantee? category? maintenance? minuscule? privilege? restaurant? rhythm? separate? license? noticeable? occurrence? ✎

19. Weird and Wonderful Words: Highlights from a Series of Posts

(11-8-13, 12-21-13, 1-23-14, 3-26-14,
6-26-14, 11-14-14, 11-19-14, 12-3-14,
12-19-14, 1-2-15, and 1-9-15)

A few years ago, one of my seventh grade students told me about this great word she had learned (I don't know where she had learned it). The word was *defenestrate*, which means to throw something or someone out of a window. This was a new word for me too. She was such an enthusiastic student, and I liked the word so much, I added it to my students' vocabulary list. All the students loved the word, and I doubt any of them will ever forget what it means!

Turns out that the word was coined in 1618 from the Latin prefix *de* (*down or away from*) and *fenestra*, which means *window*. It originates from two incidents in Prague, known as the Defenestrations of Prague. In 1419 several town officials were thrown from the windows of the town hall. Then, in 1618, two imperial governors and their secretaries were tossed from Prague Castle. This event began the 30 Years War. Who knew?

So, I decided to find some other fascinating words I could tell you about. Thus, I launch the **Weird and Wonderful Words Series.**

aglet (noun)—You may know this one. I once knew it, but quickly forgot. The *aglet* is that plastic thingie at the end of your shoelace. (Origin: 1400–1450 from Middle English and Middle French).

bibliobibuli (noun)—Obviously from *biblio*, meaning *book*. This one was coined by H.L. Mencken in 1957: "There are people who read too much: the bibliobibuli. I know some who are constantly drunk on books, as other men are drunk on whiskey or religion. They wander through this most diverting and stimulating of worlds in a haze, seeing nothing and hearing nothing." So there! Proud to be one!

cataglottism (noun)—This one, like *bibliobibuli,* is in the *Urban Dictionary.* It is from the Greek *cato (*down*) and glotta/glossa* (tongue). You figure it out! Seriously, it means French kissing.

discalced (adjective)—This word means *barefooted*, usually referring to friars and nuns who wear sandals. (Origin: 1625 from the Latin)

epeolatry (noun)—Of course, I especially like this one, which means *the worship of words.* It comes from *epos*, which means *word* in Greek, and was apparently coined in 1860 by Oliver Wendell Holmes, Sr.

funambulists (noun)—Tightrope walkers. (I get the *ambulist* part, but the *fun*??)

gound (noun)—The gunk that collects in the corners of the eyes during sleep. (Now you know.)

hircine (adjective)—Goat-like; also, lustful. (You've heard of *canine, feline, equine, porcine*—I guess this is the *goat* one!)

iatrarchy (noun)—You have heard of *matriarchy, hierarchy,* and *monarchy.* Well, *iatrarchy* is a government run by physicians. Good idea or no?? Don't get this one confused with *kakistrocracy,* which is a "government run by the worst people." I guess you need to figure out for yourself who *those* people are.

jackanapes (noun)—I remember this one from a Shakespeare Insult Sheet I used to hand out to my students after we finished reading *Julius Caesar,* so I assume this word was coined by the Bard himself. It means an impudent child or conceited fellow.

kickie-wickie (noun)—Another of Shakespeare's originals. It means *wife* and is apparently not a valid word in Scrabble.

latrinalia (noun)—Graffiti found in restrooms

mammothrept (noun)—A spoiled child

neophobia (noun)—A fear of novelty

onychophagy (noun)—The habit of biting one's fingernails

parorexia (noun)—A desire to eat strange food

qualtagh (noun)—The first person you see after leaving your house

rackensak (noun)—Who knew that a rackensak is a native of Arkansas? I didn't!

se (noun)—Twenty-five stringed Chinese zither (Scrabble word?)

textrovert (noun)—One who feels much braver when communicating by text message rather than in person (This is obviously a new word and is in the urban dictionary . . . and aren't most people textroverts?? Add this one to Meyer Briggs!)

uxorious (adjective)—Excessively fond of one's own wife (Aw, sweet . . .)

vigintiquintuple (noun)—Result of multiplying by twenty-five

whiskerando (noun)—A whiskered person (*I love this one!*)

xanthippe (noun)—Ill-tempered woman

yob (noun)—Hoodlum

zenzizenzizenzic (noun)—Eighth power of a number. This HAS to be my favorite! ✎

20. *etc., i.e., e.g.—* What's Up with These?

(1-17-14)

Most people know what *etc.* means, but sometimes *i.e.* and *e.g.* can be confusing. They are all Latin phrases, and here are the translations:

- *etc.*—*et cetera*—means **and others**
- *e.g.*—*exempli gratia*—means **for example**
- *i.e.*—*id est*—means **that is**

1. etc.—Used at the end of a list in text.

- The wedding had an Italian menu, which consisted of pasta, pizza, lasagna, cannelloni, etc.

Etc. is often best avoided, especially in text. It is fine in a table or chart. Alternatives are to just say **and others** or **and more,** or just to list everything. Sometimes you can even use **for example** instead:

- The wedding had an Italian menu, for example, pasta, pizza, lasagna, and cannelloni.

2. e.g.—Used instead of **for example.**

Once again *e.g.* is best avoided, particularly in formal writing, although it is fine in charts and tables. Why not just say **for example**? If you want to use *e.g.,* make sure you put periods after both letters, and commas before and after the expression. Do not put *e.g.* in italics or bold or quotes. (I am doing so because I am using it as itself here, and I also want it to stand out.) If you are putting a complete sentence after *e.g.* or *for example*, you can put a semicolon between the sentences. You can also put *e.g.* in parentheses. All the following examples are correct.

- The wedding had an Italian theme, **e.g.,** the menu was completely Italian. (You could also use a semicolon before *e.g.*)

- The wedding had an Italian theme, **for example**, all Italian food.

- The wedding had an Italian theme; **for example**, all the food was Italian.

- The wedding had an Italian theme (e.g., the menu was completely Italian).

3. i.e.—Used instead of *that is.*

The exact same punctuation rules apply to both *i.e.* and *e.g.* Use a period after each letter and a comma before and after the expression. If a complete sentence follows the expression, you can use a semicolon rather than a comma before it. Of course, you could use a period instead of the semicolon, but you aren't afraid of semicolons anymore, right?

You can also spell it out instead of using *i.e.*, and you can put it in parentheses. **However, i.e. doesn't mean the same thing as e.g., and they are not interchangeable—usually.** (Sometimes they are pretty close.)

- I am taking two languages this year, *i.e.,* Spanish and Italian.

In the above sentence, **e.g.** would be incorrect. You are **not** using Spanish and Italian as examples. Instead, you are explaining that you are taking two languages by telling what they are. Notice that *i.e.* is really an equal sign (the two languages equal Spanish and Italian).

- I am proud that my son is the drum major for the band; *i.e.,* he is leading the marching band.

In the above sentence you are explaining what you mean by *drum major.* Once again, you see that *i.e.* is an equal sign, saying that drum major equals the person who leads the marching band.

Simple? ✎

21. Confusing Words: Highlights from a Series of Posts

(4-11-14, 4-19-14, 4-25-14, 5-2-14, 5-7-14,
5-15-14, 5-22-14, 6-6-14, 6-12-14)

There are many, many commonly confused words; they are covered in my books and in my blog posts. Since this is a summary of several posts, I chose some of the most common ones. For the complete list, see the actual blog posts on my website or check *The Best Grammar Workbook Ever!* In alphabetical order, here we go:

Affect/Effect: This troublesome pair is the granddaddy of troublesome! These two words are different parts of speech. *Affect* is a verb, an action. *Effect* is a noun, a thing. You can put an article in front of *effect* (*the* effect, *an* effect).

- *The hot weather has a positive **effect** on my mood.*

- *The hot weather **affects** me and improves my mood.*

Alright/All right: This one is easy. Always use **all right** as two words. *Alright* isn't a word (or is a really slang word, so avoid it).

- *Everything will be **all right.***

- ***All right.** I will go with you.*

Anyway/Anyways: NO, *anyways* is not the plural of *anyway* (just kidding)! There is no *anyways*. That goes for *anywhere, everywhere,* and *somewhere*. There are no *anywheres, everywheres,* or *somewheres*.

Bring/Take: These two words go in opposite directions. You *take* something away, but you *bring* it back.

Capital/Capitol: Usually the word you want is *capital* with an *al*. It is *capital* letters, and Sacramento is the *capital* of California. *Capitol* with an *ol* is used to refer to the actual Capitol building.

Desert/Dessert: There are three of these to confuse. There is the sweet one, the dry one, and the lonely one. Here they are, used correctly:

- I want chocolate cake for ***dessert.***

- It is too hot for me in the ***desert.***

- If you **desert** your fellow soldiers, you will be in big trouble. (Pronounced that same as the sweet one.)

Disinterested/Uninterested: If you don't like watching baseball or football, you are probably ***uninterested*** in sports (***not*** interested). If you are judging a competition, we hope you are ***disinterested*** (impartial, having no interest in who wins.)

- I am ***uninterested*** in reading about history.

- We need a ***disinterested*** person to decide which team will go first.

Farther/Further: Farther has to do with *distance*. **Further** means *any more*.

- *I live **farther** away from the college than you do.*

- *I cannot talk about this any **further** today.*

Hanged/Hung: Let's say that today I am **hanging** a picture. Yesterday, I ***hung*** a picture. Yesterday, I also ***hung*** the laundry out to dry. (Oh, yes, we all have dryers these days . . . well, a bunch of years ago.) But yesterday, they ***hanged*** a man. ***Hanged*** is used as the past tense of ***hang*** only when there is a noose involved.

Imply/Infer: These two words are sort of opposites and go in different directions. ***Imply*** means to suggest or hint at something without coming right out and saying it. So you might ***imply*** by your smile that you are happy. Someone looking at you would see your smile and ***infer*** that you are happy. So ***implying*** is sending the information out, and **inferring** is taking the information in.

Lay/Lie—If you are going to use ***lay,*** you need an object. In other words, you need to ***lay*** something.

- I am going to ***lie*** on the sofa.

- I am going to **lay my purse** on the sofa.

It gets more confusing in the other tenses:

- Yesterday, I ***lay*** on the sofa.

- Yesterday, I ***laid my purse*** on the sofa.

- Every day this week, I ***have lain*** on the sofa.

- Every day this week, I ***have laid my purse*** on the sofa.

Passed/Past—***Passed*** is the past tense of the verb ***to pass.*** ***Past*** is a preposition.

- We *passed* the church on our way to school. (verb)

- We went *past the church* on our way to school. (preposition)

Precede/Proceed—*Precede* means "to come before" something else. *Proceed* means "to continue along." *Procede* isn't a word.

- The rally will *precede* the game.

- The parade will *proceed* down Main Street.

Principal/Principle—There are actually *four* meanings of these words: *three* of them are spelled *principal,* and only one is spelled *principle*.

- There is a new *principal* of the high school. (head of a school)

- I need to figure out the *principal* and interest of my mortgage. (financial meaning)

- I received a *principal* role in the play. (the only *adjective* in the four; means *the main one*)

- It is against my *principles* to lie. (rule or ethic)

Stationary/Stationery—The one that ends in *ary* means "standing still." You remember this by remembering that there is an *a* in *place* (standing in place). Yes, there is also an *e* in *place,* but it is silent! The one ending in *ery* is the pretty paper. Does anyone use it anymore?

- I just bought a *stationary* bike.

- My *stationery* has pretty pink flowers on it.

Then/Than—***Then*** is an adverb and refers to time. ***Than*** is used for comparison. Much of the time the wrong one indicates a typo.

- Now and ***then*** I eat chocolate.

- Chocolate is better ***than*** wheatgrass.

There/Their/They're—Yes, this one is still sometimes written incorrectly!

- ***There*** is a place: Go sit over ***there.***

- ***Their*** is possessive: I am ***their*** mother.

- ***They're*** is a contraction meaning ***they are. They're*** with their mother over there.

Toward/Towards—Use either one. They are the same, except Americans generally drop the *s*; the British use the *s*.

Whose/Who's—***Whose*** is possessive. ***Who's*** is a contraction that means ***who is***.

- ***Whose*** package is this?

- It belongs to the man ***who's*** in the front row.

Your/You're—Same as ***whose*** and ***who's***. ***Your*** is possessive. ***You're*** is a contraction that means ***you are***.

- Is this ***your*** package?

- Yes, ***you're*** correct. ✎

22. Our Top Pronunciation Peeves

(2-7-15)

When I asked readers for their top grammar peeves, some of these peeves had to do with pronunciation, so this blog post will be about those. We all know about *Febuary* and *liberry* . . . so check these out:

Wait! Is your top pronunciation peeve, people who pronounce *pronunciation* as *pronounciation* (and spell it that way too)?

My top pronunciation peeve is the one that 99 percent of my students say: ***mischeevious,*** with the accent on the second syllable (instead of the first) and the last syllable pronounced as ***eeus*** rather than just ***us***. And many adults say it that way too! Drives me nuts. But enough about me. Here are some of your pronunciation peeves:

1. ***acrost***—instead of ***across***. I have heard this one more than once!

2. ***CONtribute***—with the accent on the first syllable rather than the second. I must say I had never noticed this one until I heard it on the radio just today.

3. ***idear***—instead of ***idea***. But isn't that just an accent issue? (Hello, Bostonians!)

4. **perspective**—instead of **prospective,** seen in a newspaper, so obviously this one is just a confusion between two words. OK, not really pronunciation.

5. **phertographer**—instead of **photographer.** Hey, look at that **pherto**!

6. **heighth**—instead of **height.** **Width** ends in **th,** but **height** doesn't!

7. **ta**—instead of **to.** Send it **ta** me, will **ya**?

8. **realator**—instead of **realtor.** Two syllables, not three.

9. **reprize**—instead of **reprise** (repreeze). It is **reprisal** (reprizal) but not **reprize.**

10. **tempature**—instead of **temperature** . . . especially if said by a meteorologist.

11. dropped **g**s at the end of words—a pretty common one! I don't know if I'm **comin'** or **goin'.**

12. **often** pronounced with the **t**—I like the **t** silent! That is one of mine!

Then, there is **jew-lery** instead of **jewel-ry** (new branch of Judaism?) (I am Jewish; I can make a joke!) ✎

Part Four

Posts About Writing Style

23. Jabberwocky Gibberish?

(3-31-13)

Have you ever really tried to read your mortgage papers? How about the income tax instructions? The fine print on your credit card? Is there really a reason to write that way?

Writing is a form of communication, so if you aren't communicating, you aren't writing well! There is no need to use a big word when a small one will do. There is no need to use a long sentence when a short one will do.

Here are some tips for writing effectively (if you are writing a novel, some of these may not apply!):

1. Short words usually have more punch than long words.

2. Words have more punch when placed at the end of a sentence, so you might try rearranging your sentence to put the important word at the end if you can.

3. A good way to proofread your writing is to read it aloud to yourself.

4. When writing an e-mail, always proof it before you hit Send. There are two reasons for this: First, you want to make sure you have proofread it, and it is correct. Second, you want to make sure you want to send it; in fact, some suggest that you leave out the TO line until you are sure it is

appropriate to send. E-mails sent in a moment of emotion are never good things!

5. Use the active voice most of the time. (In the active voice the subject is the **doer**.) For example: **She drove the car** (active) rather than **The car was driven by her** (passive).

6. Short sentences are often stronger and more effective than longer ones. However, it is best to mix short and long sentences. Sentences that are all the same length will make your writing seem choppy and grade-schoolish.

7. Generally, sentences should be between about 15 and 23 words.

8. Start about two-thirds of your sentences with the subject, rather than with an introductory phrase or clause.

9. Remember that spell check doesn't catch everything (for example, a word that is actually a word, but not the right word for the sentence).

10. If you use *this* or *it*, make sure your reader is clear about what you are referring to. ✎

24. Italics vs. Quotation Marks

(5-9-13)

You are writing a book title, and you wonder whether you should put it in italics or quotation marks. What about a newspaper article? Yes, there are standards, and they are not difficult.

In general, **big things go in italics, and parts of those things go in quotation marks**. If you are writing by hand (does anyone even do that anymore?), you can't do italics (no, really you can't), so you underline instead. If, however, you're typing and can use italics, use italics rather than underlining.

The following things should be in italics or underlined (please, not both!):

- Book titles, magazine titles, newspaper names, movie titles, TV show titles, CD titles, pieces of art, operas, play titles, and even boats and airplanes (if you happen to give your boat or plane a name).

The following things should be in quotation marks: (These should be double quotes, not single, unless you are quoting something within something already in quotes).

- Chapter titles, articles in magazines and newspapers, TV episode titles, song titles, arias in operas, and any names of scenes or acts in a play.

Next question: Which words are capitalized in titles, anyway? Next blog post! ✎

25. Capitalization in Titles: Which Words?

(5-17-13)

Headings, chapter titles, book titles, movie titles . . . These titles all require proper capitalization. Which words are capitalized in a title, anyway? Which words are not?

Here are some rules to help you:

1. The first and last words of a title are **always** capitalized, no matter what they are.

2. The articles *a, and,* and *the* are *not* capitalized unless they are the first or last words of a title.

3. The conjunctions *for, and, nor, but, or, yet,* and *so* are not capitalized unless they are the first or last words of a title. However, sometimes *for, yet,* and *so* can be other parts of speech. *For* can also be a preposition, but you don't have to worry about that because little prepositions are not capitalized either! However, *yet* and *so* can also be adverbs, and adverbs *are* capitalized in a title. Here are some examples of *yet* and *so*:

- I am so tired. (*So* is an adverb.)

- I am tired, so I will take a nap. (*So* is a conjunction here; it is connecting two clauses.)

- Are we there yet? (***Yet*** is an adverb here.)

- I am tired, yet I can't sleep. (***Yet*** is a conjunction here, a connecting word.)

You probably won't have to worry about ***yet*** and ***so*** too much in titles. My guess is usually they will be adverbs in a title, unless your title is really long. So capitalize them.

4. Small prepositions of four or fewer letters (with four letters you have a choice of whether or not to capitalize) are not capitalized unless they are the first word of a title.

- Common short prepositions: *to, for, by, in, out, up, down, at, with, past, over.*

- Common longer prepositions (capitalize these): *above, below, beyond, between, among, along, beneath, under.*

Note: Although ***in*** is a preposition, ***it*** and ***is*** are NOT! These words need to be capitalized! ***It*** is a pronoun, and ***is*** is a verb.

Here are some titles that are capitalized correctly:

- *Tender Is the Night*

- *Guess Who's Coming to Dinner?*

- *Joy to the World*

- *Somewhere over the Rainbow* (or Over)

- *Woe Is I*

- *The Best Little Grammar Book Ever!*

- *Correct Me If I'm Wrong*

- *Algebra Is Tough, yet Fun!*

I that last title, *yet* is used as a conjunction, or connecting word, so it isn't capitalized. It looks kind of funny to me. If all words except one in a longish title are capitalized, and it looks odd to you, you can capitalize all the words. In a title, 'tis better to capitalize a word when in doubt, than not capitalize one that should be capitalized.

Note: *Is, Are, Was, Were, Be:* These words are all verbs and thus very important and always capitalized in a title. If you don't capitalize these, the grammar police will be out looking for you! ✎

26. Oops! . . . I Did It Again: Redundancy in Writing

(1-31-14)

It is important to avoid redundancy, or unnecessary repetition, when we write. Redundancy can make writing overly wordy and often awkward. Read the following paragraph, and see if you can spot the ten examples of redundancy.

I woke up early because I had a meeting at 7 a.m. this morning. It is a good thing I live in close proximity to my office, so I didn't have to leave too early. I stopped at Starbucks, which is in the immediate vicinity of where I work. I am missed if I don't show up at a meeting, since the company is small in size. This meeting was about our latest project. We made a decision to collaborate together on it for the purpose of getting a variety of different ideas. The creativity of this company is the reason why I took the job. It is a great job, but at this point in time I haven't gotten a raise as yet.

Did you find them? Here is the same paragraph with the redundancy eliminated:

I woke up early because I had a meeting at *7 a.m.* It is a good thing I live *close* to my office, so I didn't have to leave too early. I stopped at Starbucks, which is *near* where I work. I am missed if I don't show up at a meeting, since the company is *small*. This meeting was about our latest project. We *decided* to *collaborate* on it *to get*

a *variety of ideas.* The creativity of this company is *the reason* I took the job. It is a great job, but I haven't gotten a raise *yet.*

Here are the redundancies that were in the first example:

1. *7 a.m.* is the morning, so we don't need to also write *this morning.*

2. *Close proximity*? *Close* is enough.

3. *Immediate vicinity* means *near.*

4. We know *small* refers to size, so we don't need to use *small in size.*

5. *Made a decision* can be replaced by *decided.* This redundancy is called a "nominalization," which means turning a verb into a noun, thus adding more words.

6. You cannot *collaborate* unless you work together, so *collaborate together* is redundant.

7. *Variety* implies that the ideas will be *different,* so we don't need both words.

8. We can use *is the reason* or we can use *is why,* but we don't need to use *is the reason why.*

9. *At this point in time* is not necessary at all. You are obviously referring to the present.

10. You don't need *as yet. Yet* is enough.

It is easy to let these redundancies slip into our writing. The best way to avoid them is to be familiar with them and proofread your work (or have someone else proofread it) to tighten it up.

Here are some other common redundancies and their "fixes."

- *due to the fact that—because*
- *I would appreciate it if you would—please*
- *with regard to—about* or *regarding*
- *completely unanimous—unanimous*
- *each and every—each* or *every,* not both
- *end result—result*
- *exactly the same—the same*
- *basic essentials—essentials*
- *refer back—refer*
- *personal opinion—opinion*
- *summarize briefly—summarize*
- *past history—history*
- *very unique—unique*
- *and also—and* or *also,* but not both
- *filled to capacity—filled*
- *difficult dilemma—dilemma* (they are all difficult!)
- *final outcome—outcome*
- *postpone until later—postpone*
- *invited guests—guests* (guests are generally invited)
- *plan ahead—plan*

- *protest against—protest*
- *repeat again—repeat*
- *revert back—revert*
- *spell out in detail—spell out*
- *unexpected surprise—surprise*

Yes, it is just another thing to think about when you write, but avoiding redundancy and unnecessary words will tighten up your writing and make your readers much happier! ✎

27. Five Tips for Great Writing: TOMAS

(11-7-14)

Being a former teacher, I am accustomed to acronyms: Did you complete your **PDP**? This year we are working on **PLNs**. Are you attending the **SST** meeting? The new standards are about the four **C**'s.

I am also used to every expert's different take on writing: **Think Sheets, Power Writing, Brainstorming, Spider Webs, Slug Notes.**

So I thought about writing and what its important elements might be, and I came up with **TOMAS**, which I presented at one of the corporate writing workshops I conducted.

A good piece of writing should encompass these five things: **TOMAS** (pronounced Toe-Maas, with the accent on the second syllable!)

T = thought. You cannot write unless you put some **thought** behind your writing. You need to have something to say, or why write? Outlines, brainstorms, lists, notes, spider-web drawings . . . all these things can help you get your thoughts down.

O = organization. A disorganized piece of writing is a mess and difficult to read and understand. The information is of little use if it is presented in this fashion. Writing needs a beginning, a middle, and an end. Writing more than five or ten sentences long needs to be divided into paragraphs. Paragraphs should stick to one topic, generally introduced in the first sentence of the paragraph. Information within one paragraph shouldn't go from subject to subject. There should be an introduction and a conclusion to your writing, whether it is a sentence (in a shorter, or one-paragraph piece), or introductory and concluding paragraphs in a longer piece. Outlines and first drafts are good for organizing.

M = mechanics. Ah, here is my favorite! By *mechanics* we mean the grammar, punctuation, capitalization, and spelling that make our writing consistent, and easy to read and understand. These components are a "given" for good writing. Besides sounding and looking better, writing with good mechanics is just plain easier for your reader to read.

A = audience. This is a surprisingly important component to writing and one that is often overlooked. When my students write an essay, I am the audience. I don't want to read slang, language shortcuts (*gonna*, 2 for the word *too, cool)*, and writing more suitable for a text message to a friend. Yes, this language is fine for a text message to a friend, but it won't do in a college application essay or a cover letter. It is important to keep your audience in mind. You don't want to use company or occupation-specific jargon if you are writing to people unfamiliar with the company or the profession. The general audience will not understand complex legal or medical terms, for example. Also keep in mind the education level of your audience when choosing words. If you are writing to an all-female audience, don't use *he* as the gender-neutral pronoun! And don't talk down to your audience! We generally don't like being written to as if we were children.

S = style. Organization, mechanics, and writing to the appropriate audience can be taught. Gathering your thoughts before you write can also be taught to a point (we can't so easily be taught how to think). But style—that one isn't easy to teach and may not even be possible to teach. Each of us has his or her own writing style. Some people just seem to have a talent for writing. Others find writing more difficult, and their writing is more of a chore. Is it possible to develop style? Probably. Of course style in creative writing (fiction, and creative nonfiction like some memoir) is a little different from style in writing letters or white papers. However letters, blog posts, white papers, and articles certainly have style too. Reading a great deal in one's writing genre probably helps a fiction writer (which is not my specialty right now, so I can only guess) develop his or her own style, as well as just writing, writing, writing . . .

So next time you sit down to write anything, think about **TOMAS**: Thought, Organization, Mechanics, Audience, and Style. Happy Writing! ✎

28. The Seven Deadly Sins of Writing:
Highlights from a Series of Posts

(4-11-15, 4-18-15, 4-23-15, 5-2-15,
5-23-15, 6-6-15, 6-7-15)

Here are some excerpts from this series of seven blog posts about the seven deadly sins of writing.

Sin #1—Run-on Sentences

Waaaaay back, when I was in junior high school, I remember my English teacher telling us that if we had even one run-on sentence in an essay in high school or college, we would get an F for the entire essay. I don't know if that ever came to pass; I like to think I don't remember because I would never write a run-on sentence. And I don't believe I ever failed a paper.

At about the same time, or probably even earlier, I remember being told in math class that we had better learn the metric system because that is what we would be using in the near future. We all know how that one turned out!

What is a run-on sentence, anyway? Simply put, a run on is actually two complete sentences without the proper punctuation between them. Generally, it is two complete sentences separated by a comma, also known as a *comma splice*. A comma is not a strong enough punctuation mark to separate two complete sentences by itself.

Here is a run-on sentence (also a comma splice):

- My sister had a job interview yesterday, she hopes she gets the job.

Fortunately, run ons are easy to fix, and there are many repair options. The simplest is to simply change the comma to a period and begin a new sentence with a capital letter:

- My sister had a job interview yesterday. She hopes she gets the job.

For those who are not afraid of the semicolon, you may use a semicolon if the sentences are related. In this case, I would say they are.

- My sister had a job interview yesterday; she hopes she gets the job.

Perhaps in this case they aren't:

- My sister had a job interview yesterday. I would hate to work in the company she interviewed with.

If the sentences are closely related, you can also keep the comma and add a conjunction along with it:

- My sister had a job interview yesterday, and she hopes she gets the job.

Sin #2—Sentence Fragments:

While a run-on sentence is too much information, a fragment is not enough. A run-on sentence is two (usually) sentences that are run together without appropriate punctuation to separate them.

A fragment, on the other hand, is less than a sentence. It is not a complete thought.

What **is** a *sentence*, anyway? What do you need to have a complete sentence? A subject and a verb usually does the trick. Of course, sentences usually contain more than two words, but the right two words will do: a subject and a verb:

- **She runs.**

- **He works.**

You can actually have a complete sentence with just one word—a verb—if it is a command. In a command the subject, which is always *you*, is understood if it isn't actually there. So when you say to your dog, "*Sit*," that is a sentence: *You sit.*

I use fragments all the time. I use them in my blog posts. I use them in my books. You will see fragments in advertisements. Fragments have a use; they are often used for effect:

- She was afraid. She made herself so small she almost disappeared in the closet. There it was again. **That horrible screaming.**

Okay, I wrote that off the cuff, but there it is—those last three words do not a sentence make. But you know that the author used it for effect and probably knows the difference between a sentence and a fragment.

It is not recommended to use fragments in formal writing such as college essays and cover letters.

Sin #3—Wordiness

In this blog post, we will show three forms of wordiness:

1. Filler words and phrases

2. Excess verbiage

3. Redundancy

1. Some people like to use words to fill space, hold the floor as they are thinking, or make those they are talking to feel smaller than a flea.

- The overuse of *uh, so, well,* and *you know* can be used to fill space while the speaker thinks of what to say next.

- Some people like to add phrases to the end of what they say to make you feel stupid: **"Understand?" "Do you know what I mean?" "Did you get that?" "Right?"** and similar things.

2. Excess verbiage can include wordy phrases, larger-than-necessary words, and more words than necessary.

- Wordy phrases can start sentences: **"What I did is . . ."** or **"What this means is . . ."** or **"The reason is because [yuck!!!] . . ."**—and even worse, using a double *is*: **"What I did is *is* . . ."** Then there is **"The fact that . . ."** and **"That being said . . ."**

- Using fancy words doesn't usually make you sound smart: **conversate** instead of **converse** or **talk**; or using words like **enormity** and **orientate.** You don't need to use a twenty-five cent word when you can use a nickel word.

- **"We will elect a president at the next meeting."** Or you could say, **"The election of the president will be held at the next meeting."** The first one is far more direct and has more punch.

- If you have ever read your mortgage papers or any other contract, you have seen verbosity in the form of **legalese.**

3. Here are some common redundancies:

- **7 p.m. in the evening** (of course p.m. is in the evening!)

- **At this point in time** is just a wordy way to say **now.**

- **For the purpose of** is a puffed up way of saying **to.**

Sin #4—Trusting Spell Check

I recently sent a text. I was writing the simple word **men.** Autocorrect wrote it as **Mennonite.** Last week I was attempting to text the word **ouch.** Autocorrect changed it to **polychrome.** I have had autocorrect change innocent words to **slut** and change **lunch** to **lust.** Lesson learned: Either turn the thing off or make sure you look at what you have written before you send it!

That imaginary friend you have on your phone is equally obtuse. If you ask her to send a text, don't trust her. She apparently has poor hearing. Always check out a text she has written for you before you send it.

Spell check is a wonderful invention. Whenever you write anything, you should run it through whatever spell checker you have available. Certainly, if you have a book manuscript, you should run it through spell check before you submit it to an editor. As an editor, I always run a manuscript through spell check when I am finished with it in case I have missed anything. However,

- Spell check will not catch the fact that *men* has been changed to *Mennonite* by your autocorrect, since spell check doesn't care what is being written as long as it is spelled erectly. (There you go . . . autocorrect. You wouldn't want *correctly* to go out to the public as *erectly* now, would you? And while we are on the subject, you wouldn't want *public* to go out as *pubic* either . . . would you?)

- Spell check will not find the pesky typos we all make: *its* versus *it's*; *there* versus *their*; *your* versus *you're*.

Sin #5—Plagiarism

More than a deadly sin, plagiarism is a crime. If you get caught plagiarizing in junior high, for example, the least you can expect is a zero on the project or paper and probably a meeting with your parents. Get caught in college, you will likely get expelled—and what college or company will want you after that? Many schools now require that papers be put through a plagiarism checker before they are even accepted.

Technology has made plagiarism very easy. No longer must we diligently copy someone else's words. Now we can simply cut and paste them.

Plagiarism is taking someone else's words or ideas and passing them off as your own without giving credit to the source. There are a number of different levels of plagiarism:

1. Copying and pasting without even attempting to change the wording. You can certainly copy someone's words if you give credit to them and quote them. There are a number of ways to give credit:

- Incorporate it into the text: *According to Dr. P.R. Jones, in his 1980 study* . . .

- Use an in-text citation in parentheses next to the passage: (Jones, 67)

- Use footnotes

- Use notes at the end of the writing

- Have a Works Cited list or Bibliography

2. Changing some words around is still plagiarism. You cannot write basically the same thing as someone else and change every third word. Just quote the original and give them credit.

3. Following the main gist of the passage, but changing the sentences, is also plagiarism. It still says the same thing, and it still is not your original idea. Credit must be given. This type of plagiarism is probably the most common because people don't think it is plagiarism.

4. Paraphrasing is rewriting someone's thoughts and ideas into your own words. Nice to do, but if it isn't your idea, it's plagiarism, so cite it. For example, you might read an article. You might then put it into your own words, completely different in paragraph and sentence structure—but not in idea. Cite it.

5. Just plain using someone's ideas without developing your own and not giving credit to them is still plagiarism. If it is someone else's idea and you steal it without giving credit, you are plagiarizing.

What about common knowledge? Using common knowledge is NOT plagiarizing. For example, I do not give credit in my grammar books because grammar is common knowledge. Historical facts, such as dates, are common knowledge. Math formulae are common knowledge. And here are the sources I used for this information!

plagiarism.org_

University of North Carolina Writing Center

Purdue University Online Writing Lab (OWL)

California State University

Remember to use safe text!

Sin #6—Inconsistency

When your writing is inconsistent, you look as if you don't have it "together." When your writing is consistent, it appears that you know what you are doing—even if you don't.

Consistency is adhering to the same standards throughout a piece of writing including format, terminology, spelling, punctuation, point of view, audience, and audience level.

Format: Paragraph indents should all be the same. Tabs should be set the same. If you use bullet lists, make the bullets the same. Spacing between sentences and paragraphs should be the same throughout. Headings should be consistently in the same font and size and style if they are the same type of heading. If you are using *italics* or "quotes" or **bold** for certain types of things in your writing, use them consistently. A consistent format is pleasing to the eye and makes whatever you write easier to read. It gives the reader confidence that you know what you are doing.

Terminology: If you are going to call a *spade* a *spade*, don't call it something else the next time you refer to it! **The First National Bank of Boston** shouldn't be referred to as **The First Bank of Boston** or **First National Bank of Boston** the next time you use it. Acronyms should be spelled out the first time you use them with their abbreviation included; then you can use just the abbreviated form. Inconsistent terminology can quickly confuse a reader.

Spelling: Obviously you want to spell everything correctly. And you want to use either American or British spelling throughout, not a combination. However, some words, particularly hyphenated and compound words, can cause a problem. Is it *email*? *e-mail*? *e mail*? Well, look it up, and use the same reference book for the whole piece of writing. If there are conflicting spellings, or more than one, just pick one and use it throughout. It doesn't matter what you choose; if you are consistent you give the impression that you know what you are doing.

Punctuation: I put this here for one reason only. Most punctuation goes by pretty standard rules. However, the **Oxford comma** (the last comma in a series) is optional. That doesn't mean you can use it some times and not use it other times in the same piece of writing. Pick one. Use it or don't. Just be consistent.

Verb Tense: Use the same tense throughout your writing if you are talking about things happening at the same time. Of course, you can switch to past tense if something happened before the rest of your writing, but don't needlessly switch from past to present.

Point of View: If you are writing in a first person point of view (I), don't suddenly switch and begin saying *you* instead. And don't begin by using *you* and then suddenly throw in a random *one* instead.

Audience: If you are writing to an audience that isn't familiar with legal terms, don't begin in layman's language and then start throwing in legal terms. Keep the audience consistent.

Sin #7—Jargon and Slang

Jargon: Language that is often specific to a certain group or occupation and is often not understood by "outsiders."

Slang: Current expressions, intentional misspellings, and other casual words and idioms.

Neither slang nor jargon has much of a place in formal writing—especially slang. Judiciously used jargon may have a place.

Jargon: You have heard it.

Businesses use it:

- We need to meet **offline** about this.

- Our team has to **ramp up** our efforts.

Education uses it:

- We need to use **backwards planning**.

- You need to **scaffold this lesson** for some of the students.

Lawyers use it:

- You have seen legalese. It tends to be wordy, unclear, convoluted, and to use certain antiquated words like *herein.*

Doctors use it:

- Medical terminology is important and a language of its own. But the general pubic doesn't understand much of it.

Jargon does have its place. First, don't overuse it. Second, know your audience. If you are writing to a general audience outside of your field, use it very sparingly and always define the terms you use. And always spell out acronyms and abbreviations the first time you use them, putting the acronym in parentheses. If you are writing to colleagues who understand the language, yes, you can use jargon.

Slang is informal. It is conversational at best. Don't use it in formal writing:

- That is a really cool idea. NO

- What an awesome report that is! NO

- I'm gonna get to that soon. NO

- What's up? NO

You want to use slang to make a point? Put it in quotes.

Obviously, if you are quoting someone, use the exact words even if the person uses jargon or slang. In quotes, anything is possible! ✎

Part Five

Holiday Posts

29. The Grammarians' New Year Resolutions

(12-28-13)

Happy New Year to all! Ready to start the diet? Or go to the gym more often? Ready to write that book? Be a more patient driver? Better mother? Harder worker? Got those resolutions forming in your mind? Or have you given up the idea of making the same resolutions every year?

Well, I thought you might want to make some of the grammarians' resolutions:

1. I resolve never to correct anyone's grammar—even on Facebook—unless I am asked. If they want to embarrass themselves, well, that is *their* business.

2. I resolve to proofread all my e-mails and texts, and especially to watch out for autocorrect. (Last week I texted a G, and it turned into *God bless you*.)

3. I resolve to let no sentence be ended before its time—with either a period, semicolon, or colon—and therefore become a fragment; and to let no sentence continue past its natural life, thus becoming a run on.

4. I resolve to give up my fear of the semicolon. The semicolon is quite harmless and has only a couple of uses. I will not be afraid to use one between two related sentences.

However, I will also not confuse the semicolon with its distant cousin, the colon.

5. I resolve to have tolerance for both *grammar hawks* and *grammar doves*—hawks insisting on every grammar rule, outdated or not, and doves ready to disregard any rule in favor of a life of literary chaos.

6. I resolve never to utter any of the following words or phrases: *have went; me and him went; between you and I; irregardless; could of, should of,* or *would of; haven't hardly; I could care less;* or *he and myself.*

7. I resolve that I will never put an apostrophe in a plain old plural unless not using the apostrophe would be confusing. This is very rare indeed.

8. I resolve not to misplace my modifiers, thus humiliating myself. *While reading by the window, my dog* did not jump into my lap because dogs usually don't read. *While walking under the shelves, the box* did not fall on my head, because boxes don't walk under shelves. *While howling at the moon, a car* did not stop to watch me because cars don't howl at the moon, although I may.

9. I resolve not to make up words or abuse real words by pronouncing them incorrectly. These words do not exist: *mischevious, nucular, jewlery, and realator.*

10. I resolve to understand that good grammar improves my communication skills and the image I project to others. However, it isn't everything. And when I am thinking about my New Year resolutions, I will remember that The Golden Rule trumps every grammar rule. ✎

30. What's Love Got to Do with It?
A Valentine Wordfest
(2-12-14)

*L*OVE—It is both a noun and a verb.

The dictionary defines *love* (noun) as a profoundly tender, passionate affection for another person. That is just the first definition. There are many. We know we can also "love" our cars, our dogs, gardening, reading, our new job, and our houses.

The word *love* dates back pre-900 from Middle English. It came from the Old English *lufu.*

Synonyms for love include *fondness, passion, tenderness, adoration, affection.*

There are some interesting words that specify certain types of love and cannot be translated into English:

Mamihlapinatapai (Yaghan language of Tierra del Fuego)—This word describes the look shared by two people who are each waiting for the other to make the first move. Oh, you know that look!

Koi No Yokan (Japanese)—This word describes the feeling upon meeting someone that love is in the cards, in time. Not quite love at first sight, but almost!

Retrouvailles (French)—This is the happiness you feel when reuniting with a love after a long separation.

Onsra (Boro language of India)—This word means *to love for the last time*.

Although there is only one word for *love* in English (save the not-quite-right synonyms), Sanskrit tops them all with 96 words. Ancient Persian has 80.

The suffix *phile* means *a lover of* or *enthusiast of*. *Bibliophile* is a fairly common word meaning *someone who loves books*. And the word *audiophile* has been around for quite a while to describe someone who is an enthusiast of speakers and other audio equipment *(love* in a hobby kind of way!)

There are many other interesting words with the *phile* suffix. By the way, *phile* comes from the Latin *philus* and the Greek *philos* (dear, beloved).

- **autophile**—A car enthusiast.

- **acidophile**—An organism that thrives in acidic conditions.

- **caninophile**—Yup, dogs! That defines many of us.

- **cryophile**—An organism that thrives at low temperatures.

- **computerphile**—Yes, I think that for most of us, it is a love/hate kind of thing.

- **foodophile**—OK, I admit it!

- **galanthophile**—An enthusiastic collector of snowflakes.

- **Lusophile**—One who loves the Portuguese language and culture.

- **ostreaphile**—A love of oysters.

- **pogonophile**—One who loves or studies beards.

- **retrophile**—One who loves things from the past.

- **taphophile**—One who is interested in cemeteries, funerals, and gravestones.

- **turophile**—A lover and connoisseur of cheese.

- **umbraphile**—One who loves seeing eclipses.

- **xenophile**—Lover of foreign cultures and people.

And that is your lesson on love. Happy Valentines Day from The Grammar Diva! ✎

31. National Grammar Day Is March 4th!

(2-27-14)

According to Webster, *grammar* is

1. That part of the study of language that deals with the forms and structure of words (morphology), with their customary arrangement in phrases and sentences (syntax), with language sounds (phonology), and with word meanings (semantics)

2. The system of a given language at a given time

3. A body of rules imposed on a given language for speaking and writing it

Who started grammar, anyway?

The analytical study of language began in both Greece and India in the second half of the first millennium BC. While in Greece it began as the study of written language, in India it included the transmission of recited Sanskrit as well as written language.

The present-day study of grammar comes from Greek tradition, where it was linked with both logic and rhetoric. Plato and Aristotle can be blamed for helping form the foundation for the discussion of the parts of speech, as they were very interested in language.

However, grammar as a formal system was first developed by Greek scholars in Alexandria (Egypt).

Thank you to **http://www.encyclopedia.com/topic/grammar.aspx** for the information in this section!

So where did English come from? And why bother with grammar?

English is a hodgepodge of other languages. Beginning as a Germanic language used by Anglo-Saxon immigrants, English also contains influences from Latin, French, and Celtic.

The purpose of grammar rules is to make language understandable. English is thought to be one of the most difficult languages to master, containing over a million words and, as we know, lots of irregularities. Without grammatical rules to define sentence structure, word usage, punctuation (we can call punctuation a part of grammar), and the like, there might be literary chaos!

Thank you **http://www.ehow.com/about_6592206_english-grammar.html** for some of the information in this section

And now for the fun part: Some fun facts about words. Did you know?

- A sentence that contains all 26 letters of the alphabet is called a *pangram.*

- The word *uncopyrightable* is the longest word in the English language (in common use) that contains no letter more than once.

- *Typewriter* is the longest word that can be made using the letters on only one row of the keyboard.

- The names of all the continents end with the same letter they start with (and they appear to be all vowels as well, mostly *a*'s).

- *Stewardesses* is the longest word that is typed with only the left hand.

- The word **set** has more definitions than any other word in the English language.

- *Facetious, abstemious,* and *arsenious* contain all the vowels in the correct order.

- *Skepticisms* is the longest word that alternates hands when being typed.

- *Deeded* is the only word that is made using only two letters three times each.

- *Queueing* is the only word containing five consecutive vowels.

- *Lollipop* is the longest word that can be typed using only one hand (the right).

- You speak about 4800 words a day.

- The Cambodian alphabet is the world's largest, with 74 letters.

- The longest one-syllable word in the English language is *screeched*.

- The word *lethologica* is the "state of not being able to remember the word you want."

- The longest place name still in use is a New Zealand hill named:

Taumatawhakatangihangakoauauotamateaturipuka-kapikimaungahoronukupokaiwe-nuakit natuhu

- The word meaning the fear of long words is: *hippopotomonstrosesquippedaliophobia* ✎

32. Happy Mother's Day from The Grammar Diva!

(5-10-14)

Mother . . . Mom . . . Ma . . . Mum . . . Mumsy . . . Mama . . . Mommy . . . Mummy . . .

Baby Mama . . . Mam . . . Mamadukes . . .

Whatever we call her, everyone **has** a mother (in body or in spirit), and likely **is** a mother or **knows** a mother . . .

Here are some different ways to say Mother:

- Arabic—Ahm
- Bulgarian—Majka
- Czech—Abatyse
- Dutch—Moeder
- French—Maman
- German—Mutter
- Greek—Mana
- Hungarian—Anya
- Hawaiian—Makuahine
- Japanese—Okaasan
- Latin—Mater

- Maltese—Omm
- Persian—Madr
- Polish—Matka
- Romanian—Maica
- Samoan—Tina
- Urdu—Ammee
- Yiddish—Muter

And some quotes about mothers . . .

Only mothers can think of the future—because they give birth to it in their children. —Maxim Gorky

All that I am, or hope to be, I owe to my angel mother. —Abraham Lincoln

Motherhood: All love begins and ends there. —Robert Browning

The most important thing a father can do for his children is to love their mother. —Theodore Hesburgh

A mother's happiness is like a beacon, lighting up the future but reflected also on the past in the guise of fond memories. —Honoré de Balzac

Life began with waking up and loving my mother's face. —George Eliot

Mother's love is peace. It need not be acquired, it need not be deserved. —Erich Fromm

Happy Mother's Day from The Grammar Diva! ✎

33. It's Father's Day!

(6-19-15)

Most of us have memories about our fathers. Unfortunately, I personally don't have many good ones. But my maternal grandfather and I were very close. Way up on a shelf in my garage is a very old little rocking chair he gave me for my second or third birthday. I have always treasured it. It has a picture of Rudolph the Red-nosed Reindeer painted on it. It needs a little reconditioning (maybe a lot), but someday I will pass it on to my grandchildren—when I get one or two!

Father—**Origin:** From the Middle English *fader,* Old English *fæder,* Latin *pater,* Greek *patér,* Sanskrit *pita,* Old Irish *athir*

Words from the Latin root *pater*:

- paternal—fatherly
- paternity—state of being a father
- patron
- patriarch—male head of a family or government
- patriarchy—government lead by a male
- patricide—killing of one's father
- patriot
- patriotic

Other words people use for father: dad, daddy, father, pop, pops, papa, poppa, poppy, pappy

Phrases about fathers:

- Our Father
- Father time
- Like father, like son
- Daddy's little girl
- The sins of the father . . .
- Wait til your father gets home!
- You're just like your father
- Daddy Warbucks
- Father figure

Some famous TV shows:

- Father Knows Best
- Make Room for Daddy
- The Courtship of Eddie's Father
- Bachelor Father
- Life with Father

Some Famous Songs:

- "Papa Was A Rolling Stone"—Temptations
- "Papa's Got A Brand New Bag"—James Brown
- "Papa Don't Preach"—Madonna

- "Daddy Sang Bass"—Johnny Cash
- "Color Him Father"—Winstons
- "Hello Muddah Hello Faddah"—Allen Sherman
- "Papa, Can You Hear Me"—Barbra Streisand
- "(Down At) Papa Joe's"—Dixiebelles
- "My Dad"—Paul Petersen
- "On My Father's Wings"—The Corrs

And finally some quotes about fathers and fatherhood:

A truly rich man is one whose children run into his arms when his hands are empty. —Author Unknown

A father carries pictures where his money used to be. —Author Unknown

Any man can be a father. It takes someone special to be a dad. —Author Unknown

My daddy, he was somewhere between God and John Wayne. —Hank Williams, Jr.

Being a great father is like shaving. No matter how good you shaved today, you have to do it again tomorrow. —Reed Markham

My mother protected me from the world and my father threatened me with it. —Quentin Crisp

My father used to play with my brother and me in the yard. Mother would come out and say, "You're tearing up the grass." "We're not raising grass," Dad would reply. "We're raising boys." —Harmon Killebrew

It is not flesh and blood but the heart which makes us fathers and sons. —Johann Schiller

Dad, you're someone to look up to no matter how tall I've grown. —Author Unknown

Quotes from The Quote Garden.

Happy Father's Day from The Grammar Diva! ✎

34. Read, Write, and Blue

(7-2-14)

Some quotes about America, independence, and other such things . . .

Happy 4th of July!

We must stop talking about the American dream and start listening to the dreams of the Americans. —Ruben Askew

America is a land where men govern, but women rule. —John Mason Brown

You can always count on Americans to do the right thing—after they've tried everything else. —Sir Winston Churchill

If you don't know how great this country is, I know someone who does: Russia. —Robert Frost

The trouble with this country is that there are too many people going about saying, The trouble with this country is . . . —Sinclair Lewis

Democracy is the recurrent suspicion that more than half of the people are right more than half the time. —E. B. White

It's not the voting that's democracy, it's the counting. —Tom Stoppard

Bravery is the capacity to perform properly even when scared half to death. —Omar Bradley

The ideology of capitalism makes us all into connoisseurs of liberty—of the indefinite expansion of possibility. —Susan Sontag

I believe everybody in the world should have guns. Citizens should have bazookas and rocket launchers too. I believe that all citizens should have their weapons of choice. However, I also believe that only I should have the ammunition. Because frankly, I wouldn't trust the rest of the goobers with anything more dangerous than string. —Scott Adams

Without moral and intellectual independence, there is no anchor for national independence. —David Ben-Gurion

The whole history of the world is summed up in the fact that, when nations are strong, they are not always just, and when they wish to be just, they are no longer strong. —Sir Winston Churchill

We used to wonder where war lived, what it was that made it so vile. And now we realize that we know where it lives, that it is inside ourselves. —Albert Camus

There hasn't been peace on earth because people can't seem to figure out that the real enemy is the people manipulating world events from behind the scenes for their own selfish interests. —James Dye

I am glad my ancestors arrived on the Mayflower, but I am gladder that there are nine generations between us. —William Lyon Phelps

Americans are benevolently ignorant about Canada, while Canadians are malevolently well informed about the United States. —J. Bartlett Brebner

You've never lived until you've almost died; for those who fought for it, life has a flavor the protected will never know.
—Anon. from Viet Nam, 1968

Anyone who has ever looked into the glazed eyes of a soldier dying on the battlefield will think hard before starting a war.
—Otto von Bismarck

You have to love a nation that celebrates its independence every July 4, not with a parade of guns, tanks, and soldiers who file by the White House in a show of strength and muscle, but with family picnics where kids throw Frisbees, the potato salad gets iffy, and the flies die from happiness. You may think you have overeaten, but it is patriotism. —Erma Bombeck

Have a safe and spirited Fourth of July! ✎

35. National Punctuation Day

(9-21-13)

September 24th is National Punctuation Day. It seems right that we should pay homage to punctuation in this blog post . . .

How? Well, I will briefly go through the common punctuation marks and when to use them.

Period (.). Use at the end of a sentence. Also use in some abbreviations. Not generally used in acronyms that are capitalized such as IBM, AARP, etc. Used for the abbreviation for inch (in.), so it doesn't get confused with the word *in*.

Comma (,). Oh, do we have to? There are so many rules! Here are the important ones:

1. Use a comma to separate the two complete sentences that make up a compound sentence.

- I am doing the laundry, and I am cleaning the bathrooms.

2. Use a comma to separate items in a series whether they are words, phrases, or clauses.

- I like peppers, onions, and mushrooms on my pizza.

- I like to ride horses, play volleyball, and knit blankets.

3. Use a comma after introductory words, phrases, or clauses.

- Finally, we are going to Paris.

- After the movie, we are going to dinner.

- Whenever we go to dinner, we eat dessert.

4. Use a comma to set off interrupters in a sentence.

- I know, however, that he isn't home.

- The world, in my opinion, is flat.

- The watch, which I got on sale, is very valuable.

5. Use a comma with quotations.

- He said, "I am not hungry yet."

- "I am not hungry yet," he said.

   TIP: Commas **always** go inside quotation marks in American English. Periods do too, by the way.

6. Use a comma with direct address.

- Mary, clean your room.

- Clean your room, Mary.

- No, Mary, he isn't here yet.

7. Use a comma with dates and addresses (sometimes).

- I was born on September 8, 1980, in Lincoln, Nebraska, on a Friday afternoon.

- I was born in September 1980 in Nebraska on a Friday afternoon.

- He lives at 45 Main St., Boston, MA 01932

8. Use a comma with contrasting elements.

- She was tall, yet graceful.

- It was a warm day, but very rainy.

9. Use a comma when not using one would cause confusion.

   - While we were eating, ants arrived on our blanket.

   - The two dresses were blue and white, and green and gray.

Semicolon (;). Use a semicolon to separate two sentences that are closely related when you do not want to make two separate sentences or use a conjunction and comma. (Semicolons always go outside quotations marks.)

- I went to college in Boston; my brother went to school on the West Coast.

Also use a semicolon (or rewrite) to clear up a series that already has commas.

- The committee included Jane Green, the major; Jim Cotton; Helen Cleary; the comptroller; and four other employees.

Colon (:). Use a colon to introduce a list whether it is horizontal or vertical. (Colons are also used in digital time). Colons can also be used to introduce other things, such as longish quotes, but not in dialogue. (Colons always go outside quotation marks.)

- Please buy these ingredients: chocolate, flour, sugar, and milk.

- In his speech the major talked about the new mall: "I think the economy of our city will be greatly enhanced by the 101 additional businesses in the new mall."

Question Mark (?). Use a question mark after a question. Question marks can go inside or outside quotes, depending on the sentence.

- He asked, "Are we there yet?" (Quote is a question.)

- Did he say, "I recognize you"? (Whole sentence is a question.)

- Did he ask, "Are we there yet?" (Both sentence and quote are questions.)

Exclamation Point (!). Use when expressing emotion. Please don't use more than one at a time. Please (!). With quotes, follow the same guidelines as with question marks.

Hyphen (-). Use a hyphen in compound words (sometimes). Consult a dictionary if you are unsure if a word has a hyphen; if you can't decide (or dictionaries disagree), just be consistent! Hyphens also split words on the syllable at the end of a line—mostly before computers. (There are no spaces around hyphens.)

Dash (–, —). A short dash (en dash, longer than a hyphen) is used in number ranges and as the minus sign. The long dash (em dash) is used to indicate a big break in thought. Please don't overuse long dashes. They have no real place in formal writing. (There are no spaces around dashes.)

- My dog—he isn't trained yet—is in a crate all night. (You can also use parentheses, but don't use commas. You might be trying to connect two complete sentences with a comma—a definite NO-NO.)

Parentheses ( ). Use parentheses to enclose additional information. If the content of the parentheses is a complete sentence, punctuate it as such.

- Turn to Chapter 5 (page 66).

- Turn to Chapter 5. (This chapter is the most challenging one in the book.)

Brackets [ ]. Use brackets if you need parentheses inside of parentheses. Also use brackets to explain part of a quote that may not be understood because it was taken out of context.

- The President said, "It [the war] will cost us over 6 billion dollars.

Quotation Marks (""). Use to enclose the exact words someone says. Also use to enclose titles of short stories, poems, songs, articles, chapters, and other parts of larger things. Use italics for books, movies, CDs, magazine titles, and other larger things.

Single Quotation Marks (''). Use single quotes only for quotes inside of quotes. Do not use them for emphasis! Use italics (or sometimes double quotes) for emphasis.

Apostrophes ('). Use apostrophes to indicate possession. Use apostrophes to form contractions. **TIP:** Don't use apostrophes in plurals (please) unless not doing so would cause confusion.

- *A*'s, 1990s, '90s (all correct).

Ellipsis (. . .). Use to indicate missing words in a sentence or a trailing off at the end of the sentence. Often used in dialogue. Use three periods with spaces between each, and if you use an ellipsis at the end of the sentence, use four periods.

Happy Punctuation Day! ✎

36. Some Real Grammar Turkeys: Happy Thanksgiving!

(11-22-13)

Ah, Grammar: The difference between knowing your shit and knowing you're shit . . .

I thought for turkey week, I would write a blog with some real grammar turkeys!

Hope you get a chuckle or two . . .

Some of My Favorite Goofs

Ambiguous modifier: Visiting relatives can be boring.

Misplaced modifier: For sale: Beautiful oak desk perfect for student with large drawers.

Shouldn't there be a comma somewhere? I just love to bake children.

Misplaced modifier: While still in diapers, my mother remarried.

Ambiguous modifier: He heard about the wedding in the men's room.

Misplaced modifier: Wanted: A room by two gentlemen 30 feet long and 20 feet wide.

Some Real Newspaper Headlines

4-H Girls Win Prizes for Fat Calves

Big Ugly Woman Wins Beauty Pageant (newspaper in town of Big Ugly, WV)

Body Search Reveals $4,000 in Crack (from the *Jackson Citizen-Patriot,* Michigan)

Chef Throws His Heart into Helping Feed Needy (from the *Louisville Courier Journal)*

Drunk Gets Nine Months in Violin Case

Eye Drops off Shelf

Hospitals Are Sued by 7 Foot Doctors

Include Your Children When Baking Cookies

A Little More Humor

Butcher's sign: Try our sausages. None like them.

A tailor's guarantee: If the smallest hole appears after six months' wear, we will make another absolutely free.

Lost: A small pony belonging to a young lady with a silver mane and tail.

Barber's sign: Hair cut while you wait.

Lost: Wallet belonging to a young man made of calfskin.

How About These?

It takes many ingredients to make Burger King great, but the secret ingredient is our people. (Yuck)

Slow Children Crossing

Automatic washing machines. Please remove all your clothes when the light goes out.

"Elephants Please Stay In Your Car." (Warning at a safari park).

And Some Easy-to-Understand Jargon!

- These guidelines are written in a matter-of-fact style that eschews jargon, the obscure and the insular. They are intended for use by the novice and the experienced alike. [From the United Kingdom Evaluation Society "Guidelines for good practice in evaluation"]

- This is a genuine ground floor opportunity to shape a front line field force operating in a matrix structure. [As stated on the "Take a Fresh Look at Wales" website]

- The cause of the fire was due to a malicious ignition incident that was fortunately contained to the function and meeting room area of the hotel. [News statement about a fire at a hotel]

- Its clear lines and minimalist design provide it with an unmistakable look. It is daring, and different. So that your writing instrument not only carries your message, but lives it. [Promotional literature for . . . pens]

- Where the policy is divided into a number of distinct arrangements ('Arrangements') where benefits are capable of being taken from on Arrangement or group of Arrangements separately from other Arrangements, then this policy amendment will not apply to any Arrangements in respect of which the relevant policy proceeds have already been applied to provide benefits. The policy amendment will apply to all other Arrangements under the policy. [Policy amendment, Norwich Union]

And here is one that truly appeared in the newspaper; it was intended as a brief description of a Peter Ustinov documentary:

"Highlights of his global tour include encounters with Nelson Mandela, an 800-year-old demigod and a dildo collector". (This quote is obviously British, since the period is after the quotations! And look what can happen if you leave out the Oxford comma!)

Enjoy your turkey! ✎

37. Eleven Reasons Why Books Make Great Gifts

(12-11-14)

The holidays are upon us, and once again you are stumped. What do you get someone who apparently has everything? Or at least has the money to buy anything? What do you buy someone you don't know so well? Books, that's what! Why? Here are some great reasons:

1. Books are easy to get. You can get them in a store or online, and you can have them delivered anywhere. You can even mail them book rate and save some money.

2. Books are easy to wrap! No weird shapes! That helps people who wrap the way I do! They also fit nicely in gift bags.

3. Books come in a huge variety of prices from the very inexpensive on up.

4. You can buy books for any age recipient, from an infant to a senior—and you can generally tell, or find out, the ages the book was intended for.

5. You can buy books for any gender of recipient.

6. Everyone is interested in something, and there is always a book for that "something." If you don't know what that

something is, there are always bestsellers that interest most everyone.

7. Books keep on giving. If you like a book, you can then share it with someone else, who can then share it with someone else. Then, you can donate it.

8. Books are entertaining. Books can take you into a new world—even if for just a little while.

9. Books are very portable. Especially e-books. They travel well and fill time well.

10. Books are **educational**!

11. **Oh, I almost forgot #11! You can make a really nice Christmas tree out of books!**

Happy Holidays from bigwords101 and The Grammar Diva! ✎

38. Quotes for the Holiday Season

(12-26-14)

Since we deal with words over here at bigwords 101/ The Grammar Diva, we thought you might like to read some words uttered by others about things we might think about during the holiday season. (Credit for the quotes goes to The Quote Garden website.)

On Alcohol

I feel sorry for people who don't drink. When they wake up in the morning, that's as good as they're going to feel all day. —*Frank Sinatra*

I drink only to make my friends seem interesting. —*Don Marquis*

On Blessings

May all your troubles last as long as your New Year resolutions. —*Joey Adams*

May you live as long as you want,
And never want as long as you live. —*Irish Blessing*

On Childhood

When you finally go back to your old hometown, you find it wasn't the old home you missed but your childhood. —*Sam Ewing*

Childhood is that wonderful time of life when all you need to do to lose weight is take a bath. —*Author Unknown*

On Consumerism

Oh, for the good old days when people would stop Christmas shopping when they ran out of money. —*Author Unknown*

Stuffocation: being overwhelmed by the stuff one has bought or accumulated. —*Author Unknown*

On December

Christmas begins about the first of December with an office party and ends when you finally realize what you spent, around April fifteenth of the next year. —*P.J. O'Rourke, Modern Manners: An Etiquette Book for Rude People, 1983*

How did it get so late so soon?
It's night before it's afternoon.
December is here before it's June.
My goodness how the time has flewn.
How did it get so late so soon? —*Dr. Seuss*

On Desserts

Research tells us fourteen out of any ten individuals likes chocolate. —*Sandra Boynton*

Always serve too much hot fudge sauce on hot fudge sundaes. It makes people overjoyed, and puts them in your debt. —*Judith Olney*

On Dieting

The cardiologist's diet: If it tastes good, spit it out. —*Author Unknown*

On Family

It is not flesh and blood but the heart which makes us fathers and sons. —*Johann Schiller*

Families are like fudge—mostly sweet with a few nuts. —*Author Unknown*

On Food

One of the very nicest things about life is the way we must regularly stop whatever it is we are doing and devote our attention to eating. —*Luciano Pavarotti and William Wright*, Pavarotti, My Own Story

The most remarkable thing about my mother is that for thirty years she served the family nothing but leftovers. The original meal has never been found. —*Calvin Trillin*

On Generations

They say genes skip generations. Maybe that's why grandparents find their grandchildren so likeable. —*Joan McIntosh*

First we are children to our parents, then parents to our children, then parents to our parents, then children to our children. —*Milton Greenblatt*

On Gifts

It isn't the size of the gift that matters, but the size of the heart that gives it. —*Quoted* in The Angels' Little Instruction Book *by Eileen Elias Freeman, 1994*

Christmas is the season when you buy this year's gifts with next year's money. —*Author Unknown*

On Guests

Santa Claus has the right idea: Visit people once a year. —*Victor Borge*

If you are a host to your guest, be a host to his dog also. —*Russian Proverb*

On Housework

Housework is something you do that nobody notices until you don't do it. —*Author Unknown*

There may be dust in my house but there isn't any on me. —*Author Unknown*

On Parties

At every party there are two kinds of people—those who want to go home and those who don't. The trouble is, they are usually married to each other. —*Ann Landers*

I am thankful for the mess to clean after a party because it means I have been surrounded by friends. —*Nancie J. Carmody*

On Peace

You cannot shake hands with a clenched fist. —*Golda Meir*

Peace cannot be achieved through violence; it can only be attained through understanding. —*Ralph Waldo Emerson*

On Shopping

People will buy anything that is one to a customer. —*Sinclair Lewis*

Shopping is better than sex. If you're not satisfied after shopping you can make an exchange for something you really like. —*Adrienne Gusoff*

On Social Anxiety

Nobody realizes that some people expend tremendous energy merely to be normal. —*Albert Camus*

I love mankind—it's people I can't stand. —*Charles M. Schulz,* Go Fly a Kite, Charlie Brown #INFJ

On Christmas

He who has not Christmas in his heart will never find it under a tree. —*Roy L. Smith*

The best of all gifts around any Christmas tree: the presence of a happy family all wrapped up in each other. —*Burton Hillis*

On Hanukkah

May the lights of Hanukkah usher in a better world for all humankind. —*Author Unknown*

Most Texans think Hanukkah is some sort of duck call. —*Richard Lewis*

On Kwanzaa

The time is always right to do what is right. —*Martin Luther King, Jr.*

On New Year

Many people look forward to the new year for a new start on old habits. —*Author Unknown*

Approach the New Year with resolve to find the opportunities hidden in each new day. —*Michael Josephson, whatwillmatter.com*

We will open the book. Its pages are blank. We are going to put words on them ourselves. The book is called *Opportunity* and its first chapter is "New Year's Day." —Edith Lovejoy Pierce ✎

Part Six

Quiz Posts

39. Testing, Testing:
Try This Grammar Quiz

(8-14-14)

How much do you know about the most common issues in grammar? Probably a lot if you have been following this blog! So try this grammar quiz. Keep in mind that this quiz is for grammar only. There are no punctuation or word confusion (homonyms, for example) errors on this quiz . . . those quizzes are coming!

You can check the answers on the next page.

Instructions: Here are 20 sentences. Some of them may be correct (but I'm not telling!), and others have grammar mistakes. Correct those sentences with the grammar mistakes.

1. Maddie is the taller of the triplets, and Andy is the taller of the twins.

2. Jeannie wished she were a princess, and she often acted as if she was!

3. Every boy on the team brought their track uniform.

4. Who are you talking about?

5. There are 103 boys in the club, but there are only six girls!

6. When Steve drove by Doug, he waved at him.

7. Either Jane or Susan will perform her original composition.

8. He gave cookies to her and I.

9. It is they who donated all the money anonymously.

10. I swam in the school pool every evening this week.

11. I feel really bad about the accident.

12. While I was at the library, I read about the Aztecs in the garden.

13. He is taller than me, but shorter than her.

14. I have drunk all the milk, so we need more.

15. I saw the boy whom they said got the touchdown.

16. Written by one of my favorite authors, I enjoyed every page of that book.

17. She looks like she saw a ghost.

18. He chose my brother and myself to be on the hiring committee.

19. These are my favorite type of apples.

20. Either my cousins or my uncle are coming with us.

Turn the page for the answers.

Here are the answers:

1. Maddie is the ***tallest*** of the triplets, and Andy is the taller of the twins.

2. Jeannie wished she were a princess, and she often acted as if she ***were***!

3. Every boy on the team brought ***his*** track uniform. (***Their*** is acceptable, but why not be correct????)

4. ***Whom*** are you talking about?

5. There are 103 boys in the club, but there are only ***6*** girls!

6. When Steve drove by Doug, ***Doug*** waved at him. (or ***Steve waved at him***. Whichever, but it needs to be made clear.)

7. Either Jane or Susan will perform her original composition. ***This one is correct.***

8. He gave cookies to her and ***me***.

9. It is they who donated all the money anonymously. ***This one is correct.***

10. I ***have swum*** in the school pool every evening this week.

11. I feel really bad about the accident. **This one is correct.**

12. ***While I was in the garden at the library***, I read about the Aztecs.

13. He is taller than **I**, but shorter than ***she***.

14. I have drunk all the milk, so we need more. **This one is correct.**

15. I saw the boy *who* they said got the touchdown.

16. *I enjoyed every page of that book, which was written by one of my favorite authors.*

17. She looks *as if* she saw a ghost.

18. He chose my brother and *me* to be on the hiring committee.

19. *This is my favorite type of apple.*

20. Either my cousins or my uncle *is* coming with us.

For an explanation of the answers, please look at the August 21, 2014, blog post on my website: www.bigwords101.com ✎

40. Testing, Testing: Try This Punctuation Quiz

(8-29-14)

As promised, here is the punctuation quiz. Some of the sentences may be correct, but the rest have punctuation errors. Correct them, and then turn the page to see the answers. (Remember that I am traditional in my punctuation!)

1. I just baked some brownies, would you like some?

2. (letter greeting) Dear Sirs; I am interested in the position of advertising director for your company.

3. I just went to the store and bought apples, bananas, cherries, strawberries and pineapple for the fruit salad.

4. Mike Jones, chief of police; Andy Crimson, homicide detective; Mayor Crawford, and Supervisor Kelley attended the meeting.

5. He tried to ski down the advanced slope, and fell when he was almost at the bottom.

6. Why did you wear that old, torn sweater to the party.

7. Out of all my brothers, my brother, Tom, is the most successful.

8. My cousin Tom, he is a doctor, is retiring next year and moving to France.

9. My dog—I have no idea how—she got there was found wandering three streets away.

10. The book that I read last week is titled "How I Traveled Across Spain in One Week."

11. I haven't replied to you yet, because I don't know if I can make it.

12. The June 12, 1965 issue of that magazine is a collector's item.

13. September, 1959 is a month I will always remember.

14. My uncle has worked for the F.B.I. for thirty years.

15. I would love to move to California; my husband would prefer to live in Arizona.

16. Did he ask, "Are we going to Disneyland"?

17. In his speech the Mayor Smith said, "It (the new shopping center complex) will help the economy of the city."

18. Although he is a famous author, (of seven bestsellers) he has lost all his money.

19. He said, "My favorite song of all time is "Yesterday."

20. He said "I am going to the movies with Jean and Theo".

21. I am bringing: salad, bread, cheese, and wine.

Turn the page for the answers.

The sentences punctuated correctly:

1. I just baked some brownies; would you like some? **OR** I just baked some brownies. Would you like some?

2. (letter greeting) Dear Sirs: I am interested in the position of advertising director for your company.)

3. I just went to the store and bought apples, bananas, cherries, strawberries and pineapple for the fruit salad. **Correct as is. You could add the Oxford comma after** *strawberries,* **but you don't have to.**

4. Mike Jones, chief of police; Andy Crimson, homicide detective; Mayor Crawford; and Supervisor Kelley attended the meeting.

5. He tried to ski down the advanced slope and fell when he was almost at the bottom.

6. Why did you wear that old, torn sweater to the party?

7. Out of all my brothers, my brother Tom is the most successful.

8. My cousin Tom (he is a doctor) is retiring next year and moving to France. **You can also use dashes instead of the parentheses.**

9. My dog—I have no idea how she got there—was found wandering three streets away.

10. The book that I read last week is titled *How I Traveled Across Spain in One Week.*

11. I haven't replied to you yet because I don't know if I can make it.

12. The June 12, 1965, issue of that magazine is a collector's item.

13. September 1959 is a month I will always remember.

14. My uncle has worked for the FBI for thirty years.

15. I would love to move to California; my husband would prefer to live in Arizona. **Correct as is.**

16. Did he ask, " Are we going to Disneyland**?**"

17. In his speech the Mayor Smith said, " It [the new shopping center complex] will help the economy of the city."

18. Although he is a famous author (of seven bestsellers), he has lost all his money.

19. He said, "My favorite song of all time is 'Yesterday.'"

20. He said, "I am going to the movies with Jean and Theo."

21. I am bringing salad, bread, cheese, and wine.

For an explanation of the answers, please look at the September 3, 2014, blog post on my website: www.bigwords101 .com ✎

41. Testing, Testing:
Try This Word Usage Quiz
(9-10-14)

This is the last quiz in the series of three quizzes. Previous posts contained a grammar quiz and a punctuation quiz. Today, try your hand at the Word Usage Quiz. The words in this quiz are commonly confused. Turn the page to see the answers.

1. (Any one, Anyone) of these dresses would be appropriate for the wedding.

2 They (emigrated, immigrated) to the United States from Italy.

3. Boston is the (capital, capitol) of Massachusetts.

4. The weather really (affects, effects) my mood.

5. I live (farther, further) away from the office than you do.

6. My husband is (disinterested, uninterested) in all sports except baseball.

7. Turn your car (in to, into) the third driveway on the left.

8. Is it (alright, all right) if I borrow your dress for the evening?

9. There are (fewer, less) girls in the class than boys.

10. The tailgate party (precedes, proceeds) the game.

11. (Almost, Most) everyone is ready to go.

12. Please (bring, take) these books back to the library.

13. This blue dress really (complements, compliments) your green eyes.

14. From the look on her face, I (implied, inferred) that she was upset about something.

15. On our way to the movies, we (passed, past) my old coach's house.

16. He (lead, led) the parade when he was the drum major.

17. Please be (discrete, discreet) when you talk to him tomorrow.

18. Kale is a very (healthful, healthy) food, but I don't like it.

19. The food at that restaurant tasted (bad, badly).

20 (Lay, lie) that blanket in the sun.

21. My (principal, principle) plan is to leave work early and set up for the surprise party, but I have other plans in case that fails.

22. Can you (lend, loan) me some money until I get paid?

23. He is the (sole, soul) person in the group who isn't coming with us.

24. I (only) have (only) five dollars to spend at the candy store. Which place is best for "*only*"?

25. You should come and visit me (some time, sometime).

Turn the page for the answers.

Here are the answers:

1. Any one

2 immigrated

3. capital

4. affects

5. farther

6. uninterested

7. in to

8. all right

9. fewer

10. precedes

11. Almost

12. take

13. complements

14. inferred

15. passed

16. led

17. discreet

18. healthful

19. bad

20. Lay

21. principal

22. lend

23. sole

24. The second choice—*only five dollars*

25. sometime

For an explanation of the answers, please look at the September 3, 2014, blog post on my website: www.bigwords101 .com ✎

Part Seven

A Potpourri of Posts

42. Typo Is (Sometimes) Just a Euphemism

(1-11-13)

In 2008 editor Jeff Deck and former Dartmouth College student Benjamin Herson undertook The Great Typo Hunt, a road trip from coast to coast of the United States in which they located and corrected typos! Their journey has now been made into a book and a blog. Mr. Deck, a former spelling bee champion, and his friend Benjamin Herson found over 400 typos on their trip . . . and they corrected about 55 percent of them—sometimes getting into a little hot water!

They did have some ground rules: 1. The typos needed to be in the public domain—things that everyone could see, like menus and signs. 2. They would not be unkind to those whose native language is not English. 3. They corrected only text, not any speech. 4. They learned not to correct a menu item until after the food was served!

Now, you and I both know that these really were not all typos: a typo occurs when your fingers inadvertently hit the wrong key. For the most part, these were simply common mistakes.

As an editor, teacher, and author, I know a mistake when I see one (or hear one)! What do you think are some of the most common mistakes in grammar ("grammar" meaning spelling, punctuation, and usage)?

In no particular order, here are the Top Four Grammar Mistakes that I see:

4. There is no apostrophe in a plain old plural noun.

Here are my vacation photo's! What?? Oh, you mean *photos*!! Don't put an apostrophe in a plural noun unless it is a number, letter, or symbol (*a's, 5's, &'s*). Apostrophes are for possession.

3. Don't use *your* when you mean *you're. I hope your coming with us.* Huh??? Oh, you mean *you're! You're* is the contraction meaning *you are. Your* is a possessive adjective (for example, *your shirt*).

2. We were all corrected to use *I* when we said, "My friend and *me* are going to the movies." However, sometimes *me* **is** the correct word to use (same goes for *us, her, him, them,* and *whom*). He gave the tickets to *my friend and me.* Using *I* is incorrect here. You wouldn't say, "He gave the tickets to *I*," so you wouldn't say *he and I* either. Between *you and I* is also incorrect. Between *you and me* is the correct way to write or say it. The rule is to use the pronoun *I, we, he, she, they,* and *who* when used as the subject of a sentence (or a **predicate nominative,** which is a noun or pronoun that comes after a verb of being. For example, "It is I" and "This is she" are both correct. "It is me" is technically incorrect.). Use *me, us, him, her, them,* and *whom* when used as the direct object, indirect object, or object of a preposition in a sentence. The boss promoted *him and me* (direct objects). The boss gave *her and him* raises (indirect object). The boss

gave the account to *him and me* (object of the preposition *to*).

1. Do not separate two sentences with a comma . . . **EVER!!** You will have a run-on sentence (a definite no-no). *I hope you can attend the meeting, it will be very productive.* Sorry, no way. There are several ways to fix a run on.

- I hope you can attend the meeting. It will be very productive. **OR**

- I hope you can attend the meeting; it will be very productive. **OR**

- I hope you can attend the meeting because it will be very productive. ✎

43. Some Quotes on Words, Grammar, and Such

(2-7-14)

Carol Burnett has said: **"Words, once they are printed, have a life of their own."**

In the words of Lily Tomlin, **"Man invented language to satisfy his deep need to complain."**

For a change of pace, I thought you might like to read some quotes about grammar, language, writing, and the English language. Some are thought provoking, others instructional, yet others humorous.

About Words

We have too many high sounding words, and too few actions that correspond with them. —Abigail Adams

He can compress the most words into the smallest ideas of any man I ever met. —Abraham Lincoln

A man thinks that by mouthing hard words he understands hard things. —Herman Melville

When ideas fail, words come in very handy. —Johann Wolfgang von Goethe

Words have a longer life than deeds. —Pindar

Drawing on my fine command of the English language, I said nothing. —Robert Benchley

About Writing

The best way to become acquainted with a subject is to write a book about it. —Benjamin Disraeli

I have made this [letter] longer, because I have not had the time to make it shorter. —Blaise Pascal

Don't use words too big for the subject. Don't say 'infinitely' when you mean 'very'; otherwise you'll have no word left when you want to talk about something really infinite. —C.S. Lewis

An author is a fool who, not content with boring those he lives with, insists on boring future generations. —Charles de Montesquieu

Better to write for yourself and have no public, than to write for the public and have no self. —Cyril Connolly

Writing gives you the illusion of control, and then you realize it's just an illusion, that people are going to bring their own stuff into it. —David Sedaris (*interview in* Louisville Courier-Journal, *June 5, 2005)*

A classic is classic not because it confirms to certain structural rules, or fits certain definitions (of which its author had quite probably never heard). It is classic because of a certain eternal and irrepressible freshness. —Edith Wharton

The skill of writing is to create a context in which other people can think. —Edwin Schlossberg

A scrupulous writer, in every sentence that he writes, will ask himself at least four questions, thus: 1. What am I trying to say? 2. What words will express it? 3. What image or idiom will make it clearer? 4. Is this image fresh enough to have an effect? —George Orwell *("Politics and the English Language")*

The cure for writer's cramp is writer's block. —Inigo DeLeon

About the English Language

Even if you do learn how to speak correct English, whom are you going to speak it to? —Clarence Darrow

The English language was carefully, carefully cobbled together by three blind dudes and a German dictionary. — Dave Kellett

About Grammar

My spelling is Wobbly. It's good spelling but it Wobbles, and the letters get in the wrong places. —A. A. Milne

When I split an infinitive, god damn it, I split it so it stays split. —Raymond Chandler

Nostalgia is like a grammar lesson: you find the present tense, but the past perfect! —Owens Lee Pomeroy

Man 1: Where are you from?
Man 2: From a place where we do not end sentences with prepositions.

Man 1: Okay, where are you from, jackass? —Author unknown

Do not be surprised when those who ignore the rules of grammar also ignore the law. After all, the law is just so much grammar. —Robert Brault

And my favorite . . .

Only in grammar can you be more than perfect. —William Safire

I would like to give credit to the following websites for these quotes. Please check them out if you need a quote on any topic!

The Quotations Page

The Quote Garden ✎

44. The Alien in Your Future—
My Favorite Post!

(3-7-14)

I now believe that aliens exist. And I believe that these shriveled-looking, green/gray, big-eyed, long-fingered creatures are a more advanced life form than we are. So, how do I know this? Read on . . .

I have been in the education field for 10 years. Many of my colleagues have been there much longer than I have and have seen many more changes than I. Generally, they say, the pendulum seems to swing back and forth, with this year's "new idea" something that they saw 15 or 20 years ago.

Progress is a given. Well, I guess it is usually progress. Let's say that **change** is a given. We see our world speeding toward ever more technology. We have smartphones, smart TVs, computers that recognize our fingerprints and our voices, and technology that does everything for us—and therefore must be smarter than we are.

There have been many changes in education lately. Many. Now, I went to school quite a while ago. And while I live and teach in California, I was educated in Massachusetts. I feel that I got a good education. I think we might call the educations we got back then "classical educations," which was a good thing—back then. We knew things: facts, formulae. We could recite the Gettysburg Address and maybe a poem or two. We read classics. We were graded on our handwriting. And our spelling. And our grammar. And we knew about the explorers and the parts of the United States government.

Enough reminiscing . . . let's talk about what is happening now. Please note that I am not commenting on whether or not I like what is happening. I think some of the changes are good. Perhaps what I dislike most is what is being dropped, not what is being added. And, contrary to the intention, which is to make curriculum more rigorous, I think it is actually being dumbed down. And I guess, why not? Computers will be doing almost everything for us. So, our job is only to create the technology that can do these things for us. Who needs the Gettysburg Address?

So, let's see . . . what is changing in the schools?

1. **Cursive is out.** Although seven or eight states have voted to keep it in the curriculum, cursive writing is not mentioned in the new standards. It is not a "21st century skill." And where it is left in the curriculum, it is taught in elementary school for a year or two, and then left. Cursive really needs to be practiced. **SO?** Well, research indicates that the process of cursive writing is good for brain development—better than either printing or typing. Cursive is also faster than printing, should your computer (God forbid) run out of steam or crash. Cursive is also a beautiful art. Back in the day, we learned printing, typing, **and** cursive. Now, students apparently cannot handle all three. Dumbing down?

2. Memorization is out. Math teachers agree that it is crucial for students to memorize the multiplication tables, although there has been talk of getting rid of that skill too. We have calculators! Forget memorizing any poems or historical documents—or the spelling of words. Facts? Who needs them? The standards concentrate on critical thinking. I personally think you need some background information to think critically, not to mention the writing and speaking skills (that seem to be currently lacking) to express those thoughts. **SO:** I hope that my surgeon has memorized which bone is which, and which medications are for which diseases, and which other medications they interact with. I hope my dentist knows which tooth is which. I don't want to watch a Shakespearean play in which the characters have trouble memorizing their lines. I don't want to see a lawyer who hasn't memorized some aspects of the law. And it is nice to be able to recite a famous poem or quote—just to feel educated. I asked my students to memorize something. Many of them were overwhelmed. They didn't even bother to try. Dumbing down?

3. Grammar is out. Diagramming sentences? Too difficult and who needs it, anyway? Parts of speech? Phooey! The standards say that students should know how to write using complex sentences, and that they should know how to use clauses and correct punctuation. However, it doesn't really say how and when they should learn any of these things. At least in the grade I teach. **SO:** People who actually grew up diagramming sentences know their grammar. Today's students don't. Both colleges and companies complain that writing well is a huge issue. I taught a group of accountants who said that about 90 percent of their jobs consist of writing! Diagramming sentences? Spelling correctly? Too difficult. Dumbing down.

4. STEM. This acronym stands for *science, technology, engineering, and math.* No, there is no *A* for *art*, and the *E* doesn't stand for *English.* This is the push in education today because this is where the jobs are: creating technology that can do the other stuff for us. **SO:** All the great ideas in the world are meaningless if you can't express them understandably in writing and speaking. Besides, someone has to know spelling and grammar to program all these technological devices that are going to do it all for us. Writing? Too difficult. Dumbing down.

5. The SAT is being changed. In 2006 the Scholastic Aptitude Test, generally a requirement for applying to colleges and thought to be a predictor of college success, added a writing test to the math and English language bubble sections. Now, it is 2014 and the writing section is being made "optional." The scoring of the test is back to 1600 (800 for math and 800 for verbal) and the writing, if done, will be graded separately. Why is the writing not required? Who knows? I guess we don't need writing. Bubbling is so much easier. This is a bit unusual because in the public schools K–12, bubbling is being removed in favor of short answers and essays on the standardized tests. Of course, a computer is going to score these essays. How? Who knows? In some of this writing, spelling and grammar won't count, anyway. In addition, guessing on the SAT used to be penalized. No more. **Guess** all those bubbles and you might just get a good score—perhaps the answer *is* always *C,* after all! Oh, and the vocabulary is being simplified . . . no more of those big words you never use. Actually, I see those words used all the times in books. Oh, what's a book? Dumbing down.

Oddly enough, I also read yesterday that the ACT, another college entrance exam, is becoming more popular than the SAT, which strikes me as odd, since two weeks ago I read that the ACT was being discontinued.

Now what does this all have to do with aliens? I thought you would never ask!

Look at a picture of an alien:

Gigantic eyes: We will be needing those eyes to stare at the computer screen all day doing our 21st century jobs, which will consist of developing newer and better technology to do everything else for us, giving us time to continue creating new technology. These big eyes will not get eyestrain from staring at a screen all day.

Long fingers: We don't need them to write, so we don't need five of them, with fingers that can grasp a pencil. These long fingers fit well around a mouse and can really work a keyboard!

Big head: I am not sure it is a big head so much as a small and shrunken body. Muscle wasting from no activity. Sitting in a chair all day in front of a screen won't do much for your physique. You won't really need anything more than eyes and fingers, anyway.

Greenish/gray color: Sun? What sun? You'd look greenish gray if you never got outside in the sun either! Your shrunken legs and body wouldn't have the strength to get you outside, anyway. And there's always Facebook if you need to see your friends.

So . . . that is the alien in your future!

The march of science and technology does not imply growing intellectual complexity in the lives of most people. It often means the opposite. —Thomas Sowel ✎

45. People Say the Darndest Things

(6-20-14)

***D**arndest??* Now is that a word? The little red squiggle underneath it tells me it isn't. But I have heard of it, and maybe you are old enough to have heard it too. (Hint: Used in a television show in the wayback. Oh, I guess *wayback* isn't a word either.)

Bu that's okay because unusual, weird, and maybe just-plain-wrong things that people say is the subject of this blog post!

How about, for example, ***all of the sudden***? I have always said it that way, but then I just edited a book that used "*all of a sudden.*" I looked it up to find that my particular resource preferred ***all of a sudden***. I think they are both OK, but what is the difference, really? It's just one article or the other one. And why not just use **suddenly**??

Here is a good one for you. Did you ever say, ***Well, that's a whole nother story!*** Ever stop to think about whether ***nother*** is a word or not? Of course, it isn't. Seems to me that it is really ***another whole story.*** In that case, I will call it a split pronoun (***another***: split into ***an*** and ***nother***). You've heard of splitting infinitives, but I bet you've never heard of splitting a pronoun!

Ever hear someone say ***It's a mute point***? Well, while it is true that points don't talk (or do they?), the correct word is ***moot*** (debatable, doubtful, or not worth talking about).

I get asked sometimes whether the correct expression is ***different than*** or ***different from***. In case you, too, are wondering, ***different from*** is preferred.

At first I thought it was just my own kids who said ***on accident*** rather than ***by accident***. Then, I discovered it was all kids. Then I discovered it was even younger adults. Maybe it makes sense because it is ***on purpose***. But it is still ***by accident***—until it changes.

I actually never heard anyone say this one . . . but apparently the British say it: ***good on you*** instead of ***good for you***.

There are differing opinions on this one, and I would guess it really depends on the context and the situation. Do you work ***at a company***, ***with a company***, or ***for a company***? All are correct . . . it just depends.

Rim and ***brim*** are both the top edges of cups. So do you fill to the ***rim*** or to the ***brim***? Grammar Girl Mignon Fogarty has checked this one out, and apparently ***brim*** refers to the **inside** of the top edge of the cup—so I guess that is why we fill it to the ***brim.***

If you dance around the pole, it is probably ***May Day***. If your ship is sinking, it is probably ***Mayday***!

Ever go into Starbucks and order a drink? (Well, I sure have . . .) And the barista asks you, ***Did you want whip on that?*** Yes, I ***did,*** and I still ***do***! Why do people generally use the past tense for questions like that? Hmmm . . . it is probably because for some reason, it sounds more polite. Don't know why, but it does.

So we aren't supposed to end a sentence with a preposition. Well, actually we can, but that was the old "rule." Ever think about ending a sentence with certain contractions? *No, I can't* sounds perfectly fine, but what about *I don't know where you're.* Think about it . . . ✎

46. A Short History of the English Language

(5-17-15)

I was so busy getting ready for my book launch a couple of days ago that I forgot I had a blog post to write! I have been writing this blog for over two years, a post sometime every weekend, and I haven't missed a post yet.

Back to the launch: Usually when I speak before a group, I use a grammar quiz, so it is interactive. This recent book launch is probably the first time I have given a true 30-to-40-minute speech, so it did take some time to prepare. I had 13 pages of notes! Of course, they were printed in 16-point type, so I wouldn't need my reading glasses.

I talked about the state of the English language and then gave some history of how it came to the point it is at now. Then I presented some things that have been in previous blog posts: funny phobias, readers' pet peeves, and interesting things about the language.

The launch went well. It was standing room only, with many seats taken by enthusiastic 7th graders! Yes, there were adults there, and even a dog! We had some laughs, we sold some books, we ate some cake . . . it was a good evening.

So where did this crazy language of ours come from, anyway?

English is a hodgepodge of, among other things, Latin, Greek, French, German, and Dutch.

Chaucer was the first person to choose to write in English, but Shakespeare was the most famous. Shakespeare added many words to the language. Words first seen in Shakespeare's plays include *accommodation, assassination, dexterously, dislocate, indistinguishable, obscene, premeditated, reliance,* and *submerged.*

Many of our common idioms were either coined by Shakespeare himself or were first seen in his plays: *it's Greek to me, salad days, vanished into thin air, refuse to budge an inch, green-eyed jealousy, tongue-tied, fast and loose, tower of strength, in a pickle, knit your brows, slept not a wink, laughed yourself into stitches, had too much of a good thing, have seen better days, lived in a fool's paradise, the long and short of it, foul play, teeth set on edge, in one fell swoop, without rhyme or reason, give the devil his due, dead as a door nail, eyesore, laughing-stock,* and *devil incarnate.*

Did you know that Shakespeare had one of the largest vocabularies of any English writer—**30,000** words? An educated person's vocabulary today is a mere 15,000 words.

The King James Bible, published in the year Shakespeare began working on his last play, *The Tempest,* contains only 8,000 different words.

The first English dictionary was published in 1604 with 120 pages, the same page count as my first book, *The Best*

Little Grammar Book Ever! Perhaps it should have been called *The Best Little English Dictionary Ever!* However, it was called *A Table Alphabeticall* (two *l*'s, not a typo!), written by Robert Cawdray. It contained *"hard words for ladies or other unskillful persons."*

In 1806 Webster published his first dictionary, having written some grammar and spelling books prior to writing the dictionary.

And here is how our language became so colorful:

Let's talk about the *Irish* for a minute: The word **brogue** sounds like the Irish word for *shoe*: the Irishman was said to speak with a shoe on his tongue! Some details of American grammar, syntax, and pronunciation are from the Irish, such as *I seen* instead of *I saw* and *youse* for the plural *you*.

Black English, for many, represents the disadvantaged past, slavery, and something best forgotten, yet we gained some rich language: **voodoo, banjo, banana, high-five, jam sessions,** and **nitty-gritty.**

Jive talk from the musicians and entertainers in Harlem added to this list: **chick, groovy, have a ball, this joint is jumping, square,** and **yeah, man.**

The first pioneers to arrive in this country needed to make up some new words. Some of these first Americanisms are **lengthy, calculate, seaboard, bookstore,** and **presidential,** with **pretzel, canyon,** and **wigwam** from the Native Americans.

New Orleans gave us words like **brioche, jambalaya,** and **praline.** (Yum!)

Gold rush words include *bonanza* (originally meaning *fair weather* in Spanish), *pan out, stake a claim,* and *strike it rich.*

Yiddish words come from the Jewish-Americans, many of whom were in the media, many of them comedians: *chutzpah, schlep, shtick, mensch, nebbish, schlemiel, schmooze, meshugunner,* and *yenta.*

There are newer additions to the language: surfer talk, Valley Girl words, and now tech words—and emojis, which aren't words at all! ✎

Part Eight

Fifty Shades of Grammar

47. Fifty Shades of Grammar: Part 1

(2-2-15)

You may think it is a cheap shot, riding on the coattails of a bestselling book and movie . . . but how could I resist? And I am certainly not the first! Anyhow, we will cover 25 shades today and the other 25 in Part 2, next week.

I have been collecting comments on your pet peeves, unusual things you hear, etc.; the Fifty Shades of Grammar posts will be an entertaining (I hope) hodgepodge of some of those comments you have provided me. So let's get going, shall we?

Shade 1. One peeve I received was "people who have grammar peeves, and *prescriptivists*." We prescriptivists are those grammar conservatives who believe there are rules to be followed (control freaks), as opposed to the *descriptivists*, who believe language is formed and changes according to how people talk (the laid back ones); they believe there are standard conventions, maybe, but not rules.

Shade 2. Some people are bothered by those who say "a myriad of" instead of just "myriad." There are probably myriad reasons why.

Shade 3. This one is mine, although I have heard others mention it. It is so weird. You have heard it a zillion times, and you have probably used it: *a whole nother*. Since when is *nother* a word? I think it means "another whole" or "a whole other." But that's a whole nother story.

Shade 4. I always thought the saying was "all of the sudden." Then, I edited some things that said "all of a sudden." Which one is it? Most people say it is "all of a sudden." I stand corrected. How about just *suddenly*?

Shade 5. Do you know how to spell out *BBQ*? I don't think I did, and it was someone's pet peeve. *Barbecue*. There is no *q* at all.

Shade 6. People using *anxious* when they really mean *eager* was a peeve. *Anxious* involves some fear or discomfort. *Eager* is ready to go!

Shade 7. Confusing *chastity* with *celibacy* was mentioned. Apparently priests have a vow of chastity, not celibacy.

Shade 8. There is a word *converse*. There is a word *conversation*. There is no word in between: *conversate*.

Shade 9: Women have been noted to do this more than men do, but maybe not so much anymore. Women tend to end their statements as if they were questions?

Shade 10: Here is a rather unusual way of saying something. Here again, let me make it clear that we are not making fun of anyone, and that many of these pronunciations and ways to say things are regional, cultural, or whatever you would like to call it: *Explain me* instead of *explain it to me*. I think I have heard this one.

Shade 11. When someone says "Good for you?" are they really saying, "I couldn't care less what you are doing"?

Shade 12. Some people had a negative thing about grammar checkers. I personally have a negative thing about autocorrect.

Shade 13. *Goed.* Apparently more common among students. And I would think, young ones at that.

Shade 14. Lots of us loathe this one: *Have went* coming from educated people. (It's *have gone.*)

Shade 15. If someone does a complete turnaround, he or she did a 180, not a 360 (a 360 would mean they are at the same place as they started, doesn't it?)

Shade 16. Misplaced prepositional phrases like "He was shot in the car." Is that near the arm or the leg? And of course, misplaced participles. Here is a restaurant review someone saw: "Sitting on a bed of mashed potato, served with vegetables, I would have been impressed with that alone." The commenter said he indeed would have been impressed seeing the reviewer sitting on a bed of mashed potatoes!

Shade 17. "I might could go." Sounds like people from somewhere say this, but I don't know from where. Does anyone know?

Shade 18. This one is weird to me. I don't know where it is said, but not in the United States: "I was sat in the chair" instead of "I was sitting in the chair," and "I was stood in the corner" instead of "I was standing in the corner."

Shade 19. "It begs the question" used instead of "It raises the question" irked someone.

Shade 20. Leaving out the article, which I know is British (??). "We visited him at hospital" instead of "at *the* hospital." Does anyone know any rules about this one?

Shade 21: Meteorologists seemed to receive a lot of criticism about their speech. Here is one: "Let's get a check *on* the weather" or "Let's get a check *of* the weather" instead of just "Let's check the weather."

Shade 22: Starting a sentence with *More important*, rather than *More importantly*. *More importantly* can be a transition word, but *more important* is a comparison.

Shade 23. *Revert back* used by "professionals who should know better." Can you revert forward?

Shade 24. You can "Save up to 50 percent and more." 49? 50? more than 50? 49 and more than 50?

Shade 25. Schools using the word *release* instead of *dismiss.* I know this one to be true. We have early release days. *Release*, however, apparently applies to *incarceration* (and murder if you have read or seen *The Giver,* who coincidentally lives in a society that is only shades of gray.)

There you have it. Twenty-five shades of grammar this week, and twenty-five more shades of grammar next week. Have a colorful week! ✎

48. Fifty Shades of Grammar: Part 2

(2-28-15)

Who needs handcuffs, rope, and cable ties when we have dangling modifiers, mispronunciations, and malapropisms! Here are the final 25 shades of grammar!

1. You weren't taken *back* by his comment (unless it was nostalgic): you were taken *aback*.

2. You are leaving the party. You say, "Thanks for having me." *Thanks for having me* what????

3. This is a real peeve of mine. There are various iterations of it, and I know you have heard them:

- The reason is because . . .

- The reason why is . . . is that . . .

- What I mean is that . . .

My favorite is the double *is,* and I hear it all the time. Sounds as if the speaker is buying time, but it doesn't buy much!

4. Silence is golden. It should be appreciated in speech now and then. However, people are uncomfortable with it, so they add filler words such as *so* and *uh.* Sometimes people use these words to hold the floor while they think of something else to say.

5. *Yaddamean?* = Do you know what I mean?

6. *Youse guys* is not a favorite—especially when the *youse* aren't even guys.

7. I am waiting *on* someone to arrive. This one must be related to I was standing *on* line.

8. Ah redundancy! How can something be *very unique*? And you don't need both *also* and *as well* together, or *etc.* and *so on*.

9. Menu items: *Good food at it's best. And martini's. Fresh bean's, potatoe's, tomatoe's, carrot's, banana's. You name it! We got it!*

10. If you don't really mean *literally*, don't use it! I *literally hit the ceiling* every time someone uses it incorrectly!

11. Cringeworthy: *I've known him since I'm little.* **Tense Alert!**

12. *Anyone who is trying to better themselves . . .* (should know that *anyone* is singular, *is* is singular, and themselves is *plural*. And we don't care that *they* can now be used as a singular. We don't like it!)

13. *Alot* is two words—if you must use it at all.

14. Based *off*? It is based *on*. (But it is *pissed off*.)

15. I fell *off* the chair, not I fell *off of* the chair.

16. Someone wrote in: My "favorite" newscaster this morning said, "The police are trying to open as much lanes as possible," right after her counterpart said, "There is an astonishing amount of accidents this morning." Perhaps there are also two job openings?

17. He did it *different*. She ran *slow*. Who took away all the *ly*'s? We want them back. We don't like **flat adverbs.**

18. *Oftentimes*. Apparently some dictionaries say it is okay. It is a variant of the old *ofttimes*. Since *often* means "many times," *ofttimes*, means "many times times."

19. *Where are you? Where are you at* (yuck)? In Newfoundland they say *Where are you to?*

20. She screamed *bloody murder*. Have you ever heard "She screamed *blue* murder?" Some of you have.

21.Don't you think that schools could make sure that their electronic billboards didn't have typos?

22. The spice is *cardamon*. Not *cardamom*. There is no *Mom* in cardamon.

23. I'm really up the *crick* now! (It's *creek*!! Long *e*!)

24. It's not *impordant* to say *congradulations!*

25. You don't graduate high school—or college, for that matter. You graduate *from* high school (or college)(maybe).

26. I know I said 25, but I can't stop! Just a couple more! It's not nipped in the *butt*! (ouch! Shades of Gray!)

27. If you are *disorientated*, you're *disoriented*.

28. A favorite peeve of mine (and people I love dearly say it) seems to be a product of the younger generation, and especially girls. Instead of ending their sentences with a question-like inflection, like some women are accused of doing (and do), girls now often end their sentences (boys too) with *so-ya* (accent on the *ya*). ✎

49. Fifty Shades of Grammar: Part 3

(1-13-15)

Well, the *Fifty Shades of Grey* book series had three, so why not three (or maybe four) installments here too? If it weren't for the continuing great responses from you readers, I wouldn't have so many shades of grammar to write about! Hopefully, these are all new shades:

1. **etc.**—Lots of problems with this one. First of all, it is different from both *e.g.* and *i.e.,* which will be discussed later! Second, it isn't *ect.* Third, it means "and so on," so don't say "and etc." or "etc. and so on." Those are redundant. Last, there is a period after etc. and a comma before it (and after it unless it ends the sentence).

I love all kinds of berries, including blueberries, strawberries, raspberries, etc.

2. **Amount and number**—People on the news are still confusing *amount* and *number*, which is similar to *less* and *fewer. Number* is generally used with something countable. *Amount* is used with something uncountable or singular:

The number of accidents on Highway 50 has declined in the past year. It is not the amount of accidents.

The amount of crime in the city has declined since last year. (But it would be the "number of crimes.")

3. **Double stuff**—There are double negatives, double comparisons, and even double possessives, and we don't like any of them!

There isn't barely enough money left to pay the bills. (double negative: should be *is barely*)

I think he is more honester than his brother. (double comparison: should be *more honest*)

This is the book of Mike's that I borrowed. (double possessive: *Mike's book; book of Mike*)

4. *e.g.* **and** *i.e.*—They are different: *e.g.* means "for example." *i.e.* means "that is" or "in other words."

I love to read scary books, e.g., books in the Goosebumps series. (*for example*)

I love to see really scary movies, i.e., I love to be really scared! (*in other words*)

Both *e.g.* and *i.e.* have two periods and are preceded and followed by commas.

5. **Elicit and illicit**—These words are really close in pronunciation, but they are sure different in meaning, so don't confuse them! They are also different parts of speech.

Elicit is a verb (with the prefix *e* meaning out) which means "to draw out," such as to elicit a response from someone.

Illicit is an adjective meaning "illegal, improper, or not allowed."

6. **Fith**—Beethoven didn't write a *Fith*. He wrote a *Fifth!*

7. **Tumeric**—As you saw with the spelling of *cardamom*, I am no cook. And I could have sworn it was *tumeric*. I always pronounced it (on the rare occasion I said it) *too-meric*. Come to find out its *turmeric* with an *r* in the first syllable. Who knew?

8. **Crayon**—So we were having a discussion at lunch the other week about the pronunciation of this word and whether different areas of the country pronounce it differently. My co-worker and I said it was *crayon* pronounced cra-un. Someone else thought we were crazy, and it was pronounced cra-yawn. Which is it? Yeah, I could look it up, but what fun would that be?

9. **Happy Birfday!**—Well, I wouldn't be happy if you said that to me on my birthday, which is incidentally, on September fith.

10. **Caramel**—Not unlike #8, there is much ado about this pronunciation. Is it *car-mel*? or *ca-ra-mel*? Personally, I pronounce it *carmel*.

11.**Supposably**—Easier to say, but it's *supposedly*.

12. **Goes**—I didn't agree with Jack. I told him the book was better than the movie. But Jack *goes*, "I hated them both." *Says* is not the same as *goes*, is it? It's *says* (or *said*).

13. Let's do 13, because it is a lucky day, Friday the 13th! So where did this sentence come from?

I just got my hair did. (Done you really, now?)

Did you get your nails *did* too? Or can you get only hair *did?* 🖎

50. Fifty Shades of Gray Finale

(3-20-15)

Thanks to your nifty comments (*nifty*? Does anyone use that word anymore?), I have one more installment of Fifty Shades of Grammar for you before we begin a new series of blog posts.

So, here we go (I hope I am not repeating myself with any of these!) . . .

1. **Compose vs. Comprise**—I don't even want to go here, but someone mentioned it as a peeve. Is there anyone who uses these correctly? OK. Here is the story as I know it: *Compose* means "to make up or form something." Often we use it as "is composed of." *The United States is composed of fifty states.* Then, we take it a step further and attempt to use *comprise*, and we say *"The United States is comprised of fifty states."* This actually is not incorrect and is a third or fourth definition of *comprise*. However, if you want to use *comprise* in the sentence, this is really the preferred usage: "The United States comprises fifty states." Therefore, *is composed of* is synonymous with *comprises*. (Got that?)

2. **Criteria and Data**—These words are both plural, *criterion* and *datum* being the singular forms. So when you say "The criteria is . . ." that is incorrect. It is either "The criterion is" or "The criteria are." However, *data* is different. We

don't generally use *datum* . . . what is one piece of *datum*? So *data* is commonly used as a singular no matter what: "The data shows that . . ."(singular)

3. **Continually vs. Continuously**—These two words are actually different, although most people don't make the distinction. *Continuously* means "without stopping." *Continually* means "happening over and over again for a long time," but not actually without stopping. Here is an example: "It has been snowing continuously since yesterday morning." It hasn't stopped snowing at all. "This winter we have had continual snowstorms." It has snowed repeatedly, but it has stopped in between.

4. **Punctuation outside the quotes**—This bothers many people. However, in British English, the rules are the exact opposite of ours. Here are the American English standards for using other punctuation with quotation marks:

- Periods and commas *always* go inside quotation marks. Always.

- Colons and semicolons *always* go outside quotation marks. Always.

- Question marks and exclamation marks can go either inside or outside depending on the sentence. If the question mark or exclamation mark belongs to just the quoted portion of the sentence, it goes inside. If the entire sentence is a question or exclamation, the mark goes outside the quotes. If both the quote and the entire sentence are questions or exclamations, use one mark only and put it inside.

5. **Say vs. Tell**—I don't know where in the country these are used "incorrectly," but there is definitely a distinction between these two words even though they both involve talking! *Telling* usually involves another person. So, there is often an indirect object in the sentence: Tell *me* that secret. Tell *her* a story. You wouldn't "*say* her a story." "*Said*" is often used in dialog: She said, ". . ." or if not, it generally has a direct object, but no indirect. It's kind of a weird distinction that must be very difficult for anyone trying to learn English! "I told her a secret." But "I said that to her." But then, you could also say, "I told that to her . . ." Go figure.

6. **Try and**—The correct phrase is *try to*, not *try and:* "I will try to make it to your party."

7. **Inflated verbiage**—This was a common peeve. Using big words when small ones will do (and often using them incorrectly or making them up entirely); using ten words when three would be better. You get the point. Some examples of inflated verbiage:

- Using words like *enormity* and *orientate*

- Using phrases like "What I did is . . ." or "What this means is . . ." or "The reason is because . . ."

- Or phrases like "The fact that . . ." or "That being said . . ."

8. **Whether vs. weather**—And while we are talking about the weather: *climactic* vs. *climatic*. The one that means "sunny" or "cloudy" is *weather*. And global warming is a *climatic* topic. *Climactic* with the additional *c* is related to the word *climax:* "The *climactic* moment of the movie is . . ."

9. **With regards to**—There is only one regard: "With regard to" is correct.

10. **I should of went**—Double whammy here: It is *should have*, not *should of*. And it is *gone*, not *went*: ***I should have gone***.

11. **Nouns used as verbs**—Many of us don't like this trend:

- Since I don't need this for myself, I will *gift* it. (Last time I looked, *gift* was a noun)
- Let's *common core* this lesson plan. (Let's not.)

12. **Overuse of trendy words**—And we all do have our favorite words! Right now *amazing* seems to be overused by many people. I have known people who favored the overuse of *basically* and *remarkable* as well.

13. **Weird road signs**—A little punctuation might help. Here are a few:

- Prepare to stop federal offices
- Semi exceeding the speed limit prohibited
- Slow deer crossing

14. **"Well, here's the thing"**—What thing?

The End. That thing. ✎

Contact and Ordering Information

We appreciate comments and questions sent to **info@bigwords101.com.**

We also appreciate **Amazon reviews** about this book and our other grammar books.

Check out and sign up for the **Grammar Diva Blog** at **http://bigwords101.com/category/blog/**

Check out the website at **www.bigwords101.com.**

All the Grammar Diva's books are available in **PDF format** from the website. They are also available from **Amazon and all other online retailers**. E-books are available for **Kindle and all other e-book readers**.

If you would like to order bulk quantities of any of our books, contact **Ingram Distributors** for print books or the **iBook store** for e-books.

And, finally, all our print books are available **to order at any bookstore**.

Arlene Miller

THE GRAMMAR DIVA   The Grammar Diva is available for

- **grammar talks and presentations**

- **grammar workshops**

- **copyediting and writing**

9 780991 167425